THE DIAMOND SOUL

5 Stepping Stones to Christlike Character

GEORGE VASILCA

The Diamond Soul – 5 Stepping Stones to Christlike Character
By George Vasilca
First edition
This is the first volume in the series titled *The Diamond Soul Character*^{TM}

Copyright © 2020 George Vasilca
All rights reserved.

ISBN (Printed Book): 978-1-09831-838-3
ISBN (eBook): 978-1-09831-839-0

Editor: Michelle Lazurek
Book design and cover: BookBaby team

All Bible citations are from King James Version,
www.kingjamesbibleonline.org

Publisher: BookBaby, Pennsauken, NJ

Requests for information should be addressed to the author at
www.georgevasilca.org

Printed in the United States of America

Dedicated to the memory of my parents from whom I heard first the words principles and moral character.

ACKNOWLEDGMENTS

——◆•◆•◆——

There are many people without whom the publication of this book would not have been possible. I owe them a high debt of gratitude. In this acknowledgment, I can only cite a few names, but my heart will always be with everyone who encouraged, supported, and guided me.

When I look back in time, I see my parents as the first I should acknowledge. I grew up in a household guided by sound Christian principles: love, hard work, and modesty. My father, as the head of the family, was the role model for my brother and I. We learned integrity, diligence, and discipline from him. He also established the rules of conduct in the family. My mother was the loving enforcer of those rules, and a role model for cooperating with other people respectfully and pleasantly. My interest and passion for developing a sound moral character has its roots in those formative years of my youth.

The second person whom I should recognize early is Amyn Dhaya, the president of Casmyn Vector Group of Sparks, NV. Amyn was a trusted business partner and close personal friend in the nineties. Together, we had many meaningful discussions on moral character, faith and religion, and leadership. An accomplished author himself, Amyn noticed my interest and passion for those topics, and encouraged me to use my gifts for writing and organizing complex material in a clear, concise, and logical manner.

The third group of people I must give credit to are the personal friends who volunteered to read the manuscript in its many versions. Special thanks to my neighbors Brad and Arlene Gill, who put in the time to look at the document. And to their son, Jamieson, with whom I had many one-on-one discussions on the applications of the teachings I promoted. The same goes for my young friend and small-business owner, Steve Conklin, who studied my book diligently. Steve skillfully used the practical advice from it to improve his personal and family life, as well as the performance of his business.

Many thanks to the following friends who browsed the manuscript and provided sincere feedback: Paul and Joanne Whiteman, good pals from Orlando, FL; Horia Maries and Larisa Pirau, buddies of a lifetime; dr. Wade Shuman, whom I met at the Morningstar Ministries in Fort Mills, S.C., in the spring of 2019.

A special tribute must go to my niece Joanne and her husband, Pete Minnie, who were one of my early sounding-boards on organizing and presenting the material in this book. They reviewed the manuscript and provided valuable insight from a millennial perspective. Loving thoughts must be addressed to my dear brother Dan and sister-in-law Oltea of Corral Springs, FL., who helped me strengthen my faith and redirect it to where it is today.

I should also recognize Father S. Vernak of Christ the Savior Orthodox Church in Harrisburg, PA; Pastor Emeritus Dr. M. Rogers of Lancaster Presbyterian Church in Lancaster, PA; and Father A. Scezki of Joan of Arc Catholic Church in Hershey, PA for their early encouragement and advice.

I want to extend a thought of gratitude to Dr. Tracy Jones, a seasoned second-generation entrepreneur in the field of personal development and leadership, whom I consider a close friend and mentor. Her experience and insight let her see the value of the message in my book and encouraged me to share it with fellow believers.

Michelle Lazurek served as an outstanding editor, challenging me to be a better writer. She also guided me through the unfamiliar and sometimes frightening territory of self-publishing. And finally, a sincere thank you to the entire team at BookBaby for their excellent work in publishing this book.

Last but not least, I am deeply grateful to my close family members without whom I could not have finished this book:

- My wife Mara Popescu, an accomplished author herself, who toiled along my side in the last two years to bring my dream to reality. Her love, boundless energy, and joyful humor had kept me going when my spirits were down.

- My two sons Adrian and Stefan, on whom I tested, to their chagrin, some of the principles advocated in my book when they were teenagers.

- My daughter-in-law Victoria, who had graciously accepted to be my virtual assistant despite her very busy schedule as spouse, full-time mom, early-childhood educator, shopper, cook, fitness instructor, nutrition consultant, party organizer, blogger, and many other roles.

- My former daughter-in-law Carmina Cristina, with whom I had many perceptive discussions over the years on applying Diamond Soul teachings to her personal and business life. And more recently, when she brought in our conversations her fiancée, Thomas, whose maturity and wisdom in approaching life was readily apparent.

CONTENTS

Introduction

"Jesus saith unto him, I am the way, the truth, and the life: no man cometh unto the Father, but by me." (John 14:6)

Lord's Prayer

One cloudy Thursday afternoon in 1993, I was hiking alone in the mountains of Sierra Nevada. I was confused, desperate, and plain scared. My heart was heavy, my spirit was down, and my brain was exhausted. The next day was payroll day for my employees, and I could not meet it. The idea of letting down a dozen or so families who were dependent on Friday paychecks was utterly sickening and demeaning to me. In the morning, I had a brief discussion with the president of the company, who told me the business bank account was empty, and no funds were coming in for at least one week. As a personal friend of mine and man of faith, he confided in me, *"George, only a miracle can save us. Join me in my prayers."*

At that time, I was in my early fifties and held a leadership position at a small startup company located in Sparks, Nevada. In my capacity as co-founder and executive officer of the company, I was struggling mightily to navigate through the stormy seas of a high-technology, under-financed, and chaotic business enterprise. My struggle was on two fronts: as a businessman, I lacked the vision of where I wanted the company to go; as an individual, I was desperately looking inside me for sources of strength, guidance, and security. Sometimes, I thought I was finding them, but in most cases, I was not. My emotional well-being was controlled by the weekly ups and downs of the company, with no stability in sight. It was not a pretty picture, and I was losing hope.

Wandering with tears in my eyes, suddenly I found myself citing a line from the Lord's Prayer: *"Your will be done on earth as it is in heaven."* As I said this, I felt a peaceful feeling take over my body. In a matter of seconds, all my worries had evaporated, and the burden had been lifted off my soul. At that moment, I did not realize it, but later on, it became clear: I had re-discovered God in all his glory and accepted Jesus Christ as my Lord and Savior. I say *"rediscovered God"* because, as an infant, I was baptized in the Christian Eastern Orthodox tradition, so I considered myself a man of faith. But as a young man and adult, I did not put God at the center of my life. My career and family were the center of it. For many years, things had been going well for us, and I was sure I was healthy and smart enough to run my life as I wished. What a fool I was!

Early the next morning, I received a phone call that enough funds had been deposited overnight and were available for payroll. I could not believe my ears! The miracle had happened, I could pay my employees! With tears of joy in my eyes, I thanked God for his mercy and said again the Lord's Prayer, this time in full. In doing so, I had irrevocably committed my life into his hands and accepted his plans. I had become a true Christian. About twenty years later, I was again on my knees before my Maker, asking for his mercy; this time, I was ill and fighting for my life. Through the graceful intervention of my sister-in-law, God listened to my prayers and helped me get my health back. Yes, my Lord is indeed the most loving, most powerful, and most merciful God there is.

The Character of Man

In the mid-nineties, I was also struggling with understanding the source, nature, and attributes of the character of man. During my three-decade-long career, I'd been confronted continuously with human relations issues for which the engineering education acquired in university did not prepare me at all. I was trying to provide answers to questions such as: How come some employees are more reliable than others? Which are the best motivational factors for people in a work environment? What about in a family setting? Can one better himself over time? All these questions were pointing me to the character of man, that elusive set of moral attributes and virtues that makes us so unique and shapes our lives in distinctive ways.

So, I started reading books, listening to audiotapes, and attending seminars about character development, personal self-growth, success in life, interpersonal skills, leadership abilities, and so on. For many years, I was spending my evenings reading and thinking about it. Why was I so immersed in such material? Because I was finding straight answers to the many perplexing questions about human nature, life, morality, ethics, and leadership that had eluded me for many years. It was a field of human knowledge that simply captivated me. As I was growing more informed, it became clear to me that the key to everything in life was the character of the person. What I was reading convinced me that people of high moral character also exhibit all traits necessary for a happy and meaningful life. So now, new fascinating questions emerged: How does one build his or her character in a deliberate, systematic, and disciplined manner? Which are the steps necessary to progress smoothly from one stage of development to another? And how much time is it going to take?

Slowly, year after year, better and better answers started to emerge, not in a straight line, but with the ups and downs typical of working on something new. The first great "aha" moment came when I understood that the surest foundation for character building was spiritual. A solid character can only be built on faith, which, in my case, was the Christian faith.

A solid character can only be built on deep faith

At the same time, I realized that the know-how, processes and methods necessary to carry out such a massive project could only be based on science. For this reason, I drew on the fields of applied psychology, neuroscience, and human behavior. I used the latest findings regarding the undeniable bond between thoughts, emotions and conduct. And finally, I added my own thoughts about the role spirituality plays in this extremely complicated and volatile mix.

As I was mulling over these thoughts and was practicing them on family members, friends, and coworkers, a body of know-how started to take shape in my mind. Once I began putting it on paper, I preliminarily designated it Stepping Stones to a Diamond Soul Character. Stepping Stones was the label defining the process, and Diamond Soul Character was the tag describing the final product.

My Late Calling

After I retired from the professional life in 2012, I could dedicate more time to the gathering and finalizing of my many notes assembled over the years. My goal was twofold: first, to focus on building a moral character based on Christian faith; and second, to construct a reliable method consisting of activities, sequences, and application practices required to develop or improve one's character. Despite some setbacks due to health issues, I recently managed to complete what I believe is a unique and practical approach to building a Christlike character, which I call Diamond Soul. It is the subject matter of this book.

When my brother and I were growing in the old country, my mother used to tell us after incidents of misbehavior: *"Dear, do not forget you were born with golden hearts which are loving, tender and innocent. As such, your heart is as precious as gold. The heart is the gift you received from the Holy Spirit, which you must honor and preserve for the rest of your lives."* At the same time, occasionally we would hear from our father: *"As you guys grow up, you must develop a strong character based on sound Christian principles. You must become men of strong faith, strong intellect, and with strong bodies."* *"Well,"* I was thinking then, *"how would it be possible to become a strong man, as Father wants, and keep the golden heart at the same time, as Mother tells us? How can a heart be tender and hard at the same time?"* Decades later, as I was working on my character project, I realized that a child's golden heart can and must be transformed during the maturation process into a man's strong character.

For this reason, I use the image of a perfectly cut and polished diamond to describe the moral character of certain adult people. I call it the Diamond Soul. There is a significant similarity between moral character and natural diamonds. As science teaches us, the raw diamond is formed over eons in the depths of the earth under tremendous pressures and temperatures. That's why it is so strong and durable. However, when a raw diamond is found in the ground, it doesn't look good at all. It will necessitate endless hours of planning, cutting, and polishing to bring it to the shape and beauty the master cutter wants it to be. The result is fascinating: a beautiful, multi-faced diamond that reflects the light in a symphony of colors. The master cutter's work has added splendor to the strength and purity of the raw stone.

It is the same with our moral character. At birth, we are gifted with a golden heart by our Creator, but then it becomes our duty to forge it into a strong yet pure character under the guidance of the Holy Spirit. It requires know-how, proper planning, and flawless execution. It takes time, effort and perseverance. But the result is equally fascinating: a strong, beautiful, precious, and multi-faceted moral character which shines the same as a diamond. However, in contrast to the natural diamond, which reflects light coming from outside, the Diamond Soul character generates its light. It shines from within. Why is that? Because the Diamond Soul is a result of the cooperative work between the Holy Spirit residing in us, and ourselves. We provide the effort, the know-how, and the perseverance. The Holy Spirit provides the guidance. Therefore, I believe the Diamond Soul should be considered another beautiful Fruit of the Spirit and a true gift from God's grace.

Concerning the phrase stepping stones, I selected this metaphor to remind me of my years as a young man hiking in the Carpathian Mountains. There, I learned how to approach and conquer peaks that appeared inaccessible. The strategy was quite simple and effective. First, I examined the face of the mountain I wanted to climb. It was typically covered with trees and thick vegetation, and with no open trail leading to the summit. Second, I was looking for rocks raising above the growth. And thirdly, I was tracing in my mind a possible path leading from one stone to another, and to the summit. Climbing the mountain was only possible by using the stepping stones on its slope.

This is the process of building your Diamond Soul character. Diamond Soul is the lofty goal waiting for you atop of the mountain. To reach that goal, you must first plan your path, train yourself physically and mentally, and enlist the help of the Holy Spirit, your ever-present and trusted friend: "Howbeit when he, the Spirit of truth, is come, he will guide you into all truth…" (John 16:13). The steep mountain is the symbol of something that can be conquered only through excellent planning, preparation, and perseverance under the guidance of the Holy Spirit. It takes time, effort, and endurance. There is no shortcut to the peak. Each stepping stone along the way signifies a new level of understanding of the Truth, a new set of virtues and character traits. It also represents a new platform of knowledge. The climb upward is a developmental and transformational process. When you reach the prize, the Diamond Soul, you are a different person than that who started the climb. You have been transformed as the Scripture teaches us: "And be not conformed to this world: but be ye transformed by the renewing of your mind....(Romans 12:2).

My Challenge to You

Dear reader, here lies the mysterious duality of the Diamond Soul character: it is a gift received from the Holy Spirit, yet at the same time is a tremendous personal achievement of yours. You cannot develop a Diamond Soul on your own as hard as you may try. Alas, the Holy Spirit cannot force you to build your character if you do not know what it is or do not want to. Building your Diamond Soul character is the most significant collaborative project between your faith and your reason to elevate you to new heights of understanding, wisdom, and closeness to God.

This material is addressed to you, Christian believer, irrespective of your denomination, sex, age, education, or station in life. I encourage you to study it, absorb it, and make good use of it. Make it your trusted friend for life. Once you learned it, share it with your spouse, children, grandchildren, and other relatives. Disclose it to friends, co-workers, and people in your congregation. Use it when dealing with unbelievers. It will become a strong bridge between your inner Christian beliefs and the world around you.

So, dear Christians, after studying this material, make good use of it not only for your benefit but also for the benefit of others and the glory of God. Be fearless--go out there and spread these teachings. Meet your

God-ordained destiny to better yourself first, then the world around you, one soul at a time, one group at a time, one organization at a time.

God bless your journey!
George Vasilca, PE (ret)

*"Build your Christlike Diamond Soul
character first, then watch your God-ordained
destiny unfold before your very eyes."*

CHAPTER 1
VIRTUES AND CHARACTER

—◆◆◆—

"And beside this, giving all diligence, add to your faith
virtue; and to virtue knowledge..." (2 Peter 1:5)

The following advertisement was placed in a London newspaper in the early 1900s: *"Men wanted for hazardous journey, small wages, bitter cold, long months of complete darkness, constant danger, safe return doubtful. Honor and recognition in case of success."* The advertisement was signed by Sir Ernest Shackleton, one of the most famous British explorers of the Antarctic continent.[1] Thousands responded instantly to the call. Why did they? They were available and ready to prove their character in the harshest environmental conditions found on the earth. Besides, they were eager to put their names next to one of Britain's most virtuous explorers, whose coats of arm displayed the motto "Fortitudine Vincimus" or "Strength Wins."

What Are Virtues?

Virtue is one of the oldest and more complex concepts in moral philosophy. It is present in all cultures, religions, and regions of the globe, from antiquity through the Middle Ages to modern times. The study of virtue and its polar opposite, vice, makes the object of morality. In our Christian faith, virtue and vice are each expression of good and evil, of Godliness and sinfulness.

The dictionary defines virtue as "a particular moral excellence or behavior, showing high ethical standards."[2] The roots of the word are Latin, i.e., virtus meaning "strength" or "worth." Nowadays, virtue is considered the true mark of maturity, whose manifestation results in virtuous human activities.

Virtues are good moral habits, while vices are bad moral habits. Virtues are habits of thinking, speaking, or doing in a good, positive, and inspiring manner that abides by high ethical standards. When we teach children good ways, we're preparing them to become righteous persons because good manners easily and rapidly mature into good morals. A virtuous and moral person is one who knows the difference between right and wrong, and always chooses right. A worthy person whose morality reflects his willingness to do the right thing – even if it is hard or dangerous – is also called an ethical person. Therefore, ethics are moral values in action. We can think of morality as the standards of thinking of an individual, while ethics would be the standards of actions of individuals.

Christian Virtues

Christian morality discusses the principles derived from the Christian faith that believers should embrace. Some beliefs have been taken from the Old Law and reaffirmed by Jesus or his apostles in the Gospels, such as the Ten Commandments brought forth by Moses to the Israelites. However, brand new principles have been enunciated by Jesus Christ himself, as described in the Gospels of the New Testament. The first two, also known as the Great Commandment, call believers to above all love God, followed immediately by loving their neighbors.

Based on Jesus' principles, Christian classical moral theology identifies seven cardinal virtues as being foundational to the nature of God's people. They are faith, hope, and love (charity), prudence, justice, temperance, and fortitude.[3]

The first three we call heavenly virtues, because their object is the divine being. Faith, hope, and charity are considered received from God, because they can only result from the grace of God, revealing himself to us. It is important to note that faith, hope, and charity are sequential virtues in the sense that faith must be first, hope comes second, and charity comes after hope.

The last four, i.e., prudence, justice, temperance, and fortitude, are considered acquired virtues because they can be sought for, and possibly acquired by each of us but only under the guidance of the Holy Spirit.

Branching off from the seven virtues, theologians and scholars have identified many other critical Christian virtues such as forgiveness, humility, thankfulness, and servanthood. Other attributes such as civility, fairness, respectfulness, and diligence are called derivative virtues, because they stem from the core virtues, and are highly visible to the society. Together, they all constitute the mosaic of virtues that make the Christian character so aspirational, different, and unique.

The purpose of the heavenly virtues is to bring us into direct contact with God himself. They have the higher meaning of giving humans the divine power that is necessary to reach out to God. This divine power is grace, the far-reaching gift that could only come from God.

The Virtue of Faith: God, in his great desire to draw us to himself, revealed himself in Jesus Christ becoming present among us. Our response to God's revelation is faith, the belief in spiritual knowledge, which cannot be experienced directly. Through faith, we are empowered by God with the ability to know him further, to communicate with him, to praise and glorify him.

The Virtue of Hope: is the response we give to God's promise of eternal life and glory. In hope, we rely on God's fidelity to his promise, and his power to bring them to completion. In this way, we acknowledge God's omnipotence and trustworthiness that he will bring us to eternal life.

The Virtue of Love: Christian love is held to be the highest form of human love. It is also known under the name of *agape* or *"the love of Christians for other persons, corresponding to the love of God for human-kind."* The virtue of love is the ultimate perfection of the human spirit because it both glorifies and reflects the nature of God. The maturity and fulfillment of one's character is achieved in loving others with a perfect, self-surrendering love. The most notable effects of charity are joy, peace, and mercy, all internal feelings that we taste deep within our soul.

How much better is to get Wisdom than Gold.
Proverbs 15:16

The four natural virtues of prudence, justice, temperance, and forti-tude grow, of course, from the heavenly virtues under the guidance of the Holy Spirit. They define an accomplished, complete, and mature Christian person. The process of maturing leads to liberty and freedom from many restrictions, but it brings with it the corresponding responsibility of direct-ing oneself. Let's now look briefly at the four natural virtues:

The Virtue of Prudence: prudence is a habit of the mind that can be acquired, developed, and used at will. Prudence is the characteristic of a person who can direct himself, with a considerable measure of freedom, through the course of life. A prudent person tends to reason out what is to be done, how it is to be done, followed by the practical decision to do it.

The Virtue of Justice: Justice is the virtue that enables us to control and regulate dealings with others, whether God or fellow human beings. Being just means being fair and equitable to others. Justice is concerned with the real relationship between two people and their rights and obligations. The right[5] is the moral power or capability of doing or omitting, or of demanding some action. For instance, men and women have the natural right to unite to form families. Other rights, named positive rights, are determined by public consent or authority in the form of laws.

The Virtue of Temperance: it masters the energies of natural emotions and instincts, particularly as they relate to food, drink, and sex. The abilities of survival and reproduction are enjoyable and necessary things in human life. They have been implanted in us by our Creator to give us the pleasure of living and fulfill his plan for humanity. Unfortunately, these emotions often rebel against the rule of reason and the human life itself. Temperance is, therefore, the moral virtue that moderates the appetite regarding the desires and pleasures of the flesh.

The Virtue of Fortitude: the human race has always valued and applauded courage, bravery, and the capacity to endure and overcome difficulties. Fortitude implies a strength and firmness of mind, which is a general condition for every virtue. It strengthens the soul of a person to face great dangers, especially the most significant threat on earth--death. This virtue controls the emotions of fear and daring, preventing one from becoming a coward or foolhardy in the face of danger.

> REMEMBER: THE SEVEN GREAT
> CHRISTIAN VIRTUES ARE FAITH, HOPE,
> LOVE, PRUDENCE, JUSTICE,
> TEMPERANCE AND FORTITUDE

What are Vices?

Vices are bad moral habits that stand in direct opposition to virtues, which are good moral habits. Christian teachings instruct us that the source of all vices is sin. Vices[6] are habits formed by repeating sinful acts. But what is a sinful act? And what is sin? In a way, sin is the mystery of human history.[7] Nothing stands out so sharply in the Sacred Scriptures as the fact of sin, which has corrupted our race. We can say that the Old Testament is a long record of sins committed by the Israelites over several millennia. Sin is also the mystery of one's own life. Sin happens when we turn our backs to God, rejecting everything that is truly good and reaching out for the worthless. Christian teachings condemn sin as evil and as the leading cause of sorrow in this life and next. Sin brings death.

"For the wages of sin is death; but the gift of God is eternal life through Jesus Christ our Lord." (Romans 6:23)

Like a virtue, a vice is acquired gradually over a while by repeated actions. But unlike virtues, which bring us closer to God, sinful actions turn us away from him. Vices attack the human nature by slowly corrupting it and destroying virtues. Rather than seeking fulfillment in goodness and closeness to God, a person under the influence of a vice begins to find his joy in sin and malice. A sinful action is, therefore, a defective human action that is not directed toward fulfilling God's plan for humanity.

The following table lists all seven capital sins and some of their offspring, starting with vainglory (excessive pride) and ending with anger.

CAPITAL SIN	DESCRIPTION	OFFSPRING SINS
Vainglory (Pride)	inordinate seeking of praise and honor	ambition, boasting, disobedience, hypocrisy
Gluttony	excessive seeking of food and drink	vulgarity, impurity, mental dullness, coarseness

Lust	inordinate seeking of sexual pleasure	mental blindness, inconsideration, love of self
Avarice (greed)	inordinate seeking for reaches	hardheartedness, injustice, deceit, fraud
Sloth (laziness)	reluctance to do work or effort	malice, timidity, bitterness, despair
Envy	being resentful to someone's luck or possessions	hatred, detraction, slander, joy at another's misfortunes
Anger	hostility or a strong feeling of displeasure	quarreling, cursing, aggressiveness, blasphemy

Underlying all sins is vainglory (pride), the inordinate seeking of one's excellence and accompanying praise and honor. Vainglory is excessive pride and vanity. Pride was the main reason for Lucifer's fall, it was evident in the sin of Adam, and it is present in some measures in all sins because it makes self the center and goal of everything.

> REMEMBER: WE MUST AVOID AT ALL COST THE SEVEN CAPITAL SINS BECAUSE THEY WILL DRAW US AWAY FROM GOD

What is Character?

Webster dictionary defines character as moral attributes or features that make up and distinguish one individual from another.[8] The concept of character can imply a variety of attributes, but it mostly refers to virtues such as empathy, fortitude, loyalty, perseverance, integrity, trustworthiness, and so on. It also implies the adoption of correct principles of human conduct as the foundation of one's character. The origin of the word comes from the ancient Greek language, where character meant engraved mark on a coin.[9]

Nowadays, many people use the words character and personality interchangeably. This is in error, because each term describes a different thing:

Character: is what is inside us, in our souls, hearts, and minds. It is a set of core principles that we strongly believe in and have adopted as guiding lights for our lives. Character is like the large and stable base of an iceberg hidden underwater, which supports the tip of the iceberg visible above water.

Personality: is the outward manifestation of character expressed in patterns of behavior that are in complete alignment with the inner nature. Personality rests on the character and is there for everyone to see. Personality is like the tip of an iceberg, visible above water, being supported by the much larger and stable base of the ice.

Character is one's true nature, including identity, a sense of purpose, values, virtues, morals, and conscience. Character is the essence of who the individual is, what he values and believes, and how he behaves. Doing the right thing the right way for the right reason all the time demonstrates the integrity of the character. This means that more often than not, one has to resist the easier wrong in favor of the stricter right. Making the right choices requires integrity, judgment, problem-solving, and adaptability. Character communicates better than one thousand words, but it takes time to be revealed. Good character creates trust and respect, attracts good people, and provides the foundation for meaningful relationships. That is the power of character.

How is Character Developed?

We all should aspire to become people of good character. But where does the character come from? How is good character acquired? Character is something that we are not born with; it must be learned. Character forms over time through education, training, and experience in a continuous, iterative process. Several factors become significant sources in influencing the character and moral development of the individual. They include heredity, early childhood experiences, modeling by parents and adults, peer influence, teachings in school, extraordinary events in life, the general social environment, media, and culture.

All this is true because the above factors contribute to acquiring almost in an unconscious manner proper and wicked habits that define us as individuals at a certain point in time. At that time, if we are honest with ourselves, we may realize that we either have a good character, or a bad character, or a combination of both. In other words, we find ourselves to be mostly a virtuous person, or a sinful person, or someone possessing virtues and vices alike. Needless to say, the latter case is the most common.

For most people, the age at which such realization about character becomes apparent is late teens, early adulthood. For other people, it may happen later in life, or not at all. However, for those of us who are aware of it, that point in time comes to be a turning point in our lives. Why is that? Simply because now we can take charge of our character through self-development, to grow it, shape it, and mold it the way we want.

But factors of great significance in character formation are extraordinary or special events in one's life. Among such unusual or special events is the coming into Christ, accepting Jesus Christ as our Lord and Savior, and the embracing of the Christian faith. Once you become a believer, you will benefit from the grace of God, who sends into you the Holy Spirit to illuminate, guide, and strengthen you.

Christlike Character

So far, all we have done was to define the character, discuss how important it is in society, and how actions define our reputation. In other words, we have looked at the character from a worldly point of view. Now let's look at it from a Christian perspective. We, as Christians, should be very focused on character because God expects us to be known as having a Christlike Character. Jesus said:

"Yee are the light of the world. A citie that is set on an hill, cannot be hid." (Matthew 5:14).

The Bible teaches us that when we choose of our own free will to accept the grace of God by obeying His commands, and when we become one with Christ in baptism, we put to death our old self and become a new creature in Christ. As Paul said,

"Therefore if any man *be* in Christ, *he is* a new creature: old things are passed away; behold, all things are become new." (2 Corinthians 5:17)

The most detailed advice Christians get about character is also found in the words of Paul:

"Put on therefore, as the elect of God, holy and beloved, bowels of mercies, kindness, humbleness of mind, meekness, longsuffering;" (Colossians 3:1)

How is Christlike Character built?

Christlike character begins with faith in Christ. Faith is what separates Christian character from mere civility or secular morality. There are many reasons for a person to do an outwardly good or moral act. However, it is not solely the outward act that makes behavior godly, but the motive behind the action that matters.

Christlike character is the product of the Holy Spirit. It is the Holy Spirit who changes the believer's heart from a state of rebellion and unbelief to faith and love. It is the Spirit of God dwelling in the believer's heart

10

that produces a love for God and others, as well as a desire to deny sin and self to please God.[10] It is the Holy Spirit that forms the foundation of real Christian character:

"But the fruit of the Spirit is love, joy, peace, longsuffering, gentleness, goodness, faith," (Galatians 5:22-23)

We can say that all seven Christian virtues are right gifts from God brought to us by the Holy Spirit, who now resides in our hearts. We can say that after the Holy Spirit plants the seeds of virtues, we should not stop there. On the contrary, this should become the starting point in walking with the Spirit to develop, enhance, and practice these virtues, as well as other derivative virtues that flow from the Christlike core of our character.

Finally, God uses our life circumstances to exercise the grace and faith he has given to us, thereby causing us to grow in Christlike character. One might say that Christian character is forged in the crucible of experience, particularly under extraordinary circumstances such as suffering, tribulation, and hardship.

"And not only *so*, but we glory in tribulations also: knowing that tribulation worketh patience; and patience, experience; and experience, hope..." (Romans 5:3-5)

> REMEMBER: OUR CHRISTLIKE
> CHARACTER IS RECEIVED FROM THE
> HOLY SPIRIT AND ENHANCED BY OUR
> EFFORTS AS GUIDED BY THE SPIRIT

This book will show you the Christian values, theoretical principles, and practical ways of forming, revealing, and applying your Christlike Diamond Soul character.

Moments of Reflection

1. What are virtues? What is morality? What are ethics?

2. Which are the seven Great Christian Virtues?

3. List and reflect on the heavenly virtues.

4. List and reflect on the normal virtues.

5. What is sin? What are vices?

6. List and reflect on the Seven Deadly Sins.

7. What is moral character? How is it different from personality?

8. Which factors influence the development of character in a young person?

9. Why should Christians desire to be like Christ? How do you build a Christlike character?

10. How does the Holy Spirit help us in building, maintaining, and revealing our Christlike character?

CHAPTER 2
ON CHARACTER OF JESUS

—◆•◆•◆—

"Those things, which ye have both learned, and
received, and heard, and seen in me, do: and the God
of peace shall be with you." (Philippians 4:9)

Why Contemplate Jesus' Character?

Who was the humble man portrayed in the Scriptures as being born
in a manger, preaching for only three short years, then dying on the cross?
Who was he who had no reputation of learning yet was attracting daily
crowds with his words of wisdom, love, and compassion? Who was he who
laid down the foundation on which the Christian faith would be built?

Of course, we're talking about Jesus Christ, the Son of Man. No other
historical figure has been analyzed, debated, exalted, or debased, loved,
or hated as much as Jesus of Nazareth. No other ideas, principles, and
doctrines on God and Holy Spirit, soul, life and death, duty, and destiny
have the power of convictions like those laid down by him. No philosophy
of life has been embraced by so many people as the Christian faith.

To best understand Christian ideas, we must know something of what
Jesus was. We need to inquire about his moral traits, his genius, and the

13

manner of his conduct. In other words, we ought to learn about his character. As Pastor C. E. Jefferson (1860-1937) said, *"this is the logical beginning
of study into the meaning of Christian religion."*[11] Because, let's remember
that the significance of what a man says depends mostly on who he is. Two
men may say precisely the same thing, but if one is known to be mean or
fool, his words make no impression on us. In contrast, if the other is known
to be good or wise, we will give him close attention.

Jesus' Character

For many centuries now, Christian theologians have been examining
the life and character of the Man of Galilee. There is a vast body of scholarly
work dedicated to the study of Jesus as man, historical figure, and founder
of Christianity. In looking at it, we decided to focus only on Christ's character as a man. Why? Because Jesus' secret in changing the old world was
his character, which he was offering to people to imitate. In his teachings, he
always encourages his followers to "Follow me, learn of me, abide in me!"

When we examine Jesus' life, we find out that his paramount concern is
for the well-being of the heart and the righteousness of the human soul. As
such, he gives himself the task of molding the hearts and minds of men. The
Reformer of Nazareth knows that the only way to begin bettering society is
to begin transforming its men in the pattern that he is. If other men adopt
Christ's character, in time, many more will do the same. Which, in turn,
will change the nature of societal institutions and ultimately of civilizations.
This is the secret of Jesus: plant the fire of faith in the soul of a man, and
then let it spread to others. Thus, he begins transforming the men around
him one person at a time, one man after another, making them his disciples

and sending them in the world to spread the Good News. This was so true in Jesus' times, and it is still so real in our times.

> But speaking the truth in love,
> may grow up into him in all things,
> which is the head, even Christ
> **Ephesians 4:15**

Let's look at several traits of Jesus' character as presented by Gospels:

- Holiness: "But as he which hath called you is holy, so be ye holy in all manner of conversation; because it is written, Be you holy; for I am holy." (1 Peter: 1:15-16)
- Love: "And walk in love, as Christ also hath loved us, and hath given himself for us an offering and a sacrifice to God for a sweet-smelling savour." (Ephesians 5:2)
- Kindness: "But love ye your enemies, and do good, and lend, hoping for nothing again; and your reward shall be great, and ye shall be the children of the Highest: for he is kind unto the unthankful and *to* the evil." (Luke 6:35)

REMEMBER: JESUS' CHARACTER IS ABOVE
ALL HOLY, LOVING AND KIND

Jesus' Humility

In his classic lectures "The Character of Jesus" over a century ago, Preacher Charles E. Jefferson[1] identifies a total of twenty-two attributes of Jesus' character. It is perhaps one of the most exhaustive studies into the nature of Christ, revealing a complex man with apparently contradictory traits. One of the most remarkable findings is that under the cloak of humility, kindness, and holiness, inside Jesus, the Humble Man lives a mighty warrior. Driven by a holy mission, the mighty warrior possesses the virtues of strength, firmness, courage, and patience, which are well-known attributes of great military leaders. How is it possible that a wandering teacher in Galilee's farmlands could be a great leader at the same time? How is it possible for Jesus to battle his enemies without having armed men around him? This is another mystery of the persona of Jesus as a leader, and we will learn a lot by trying to unravel it.

Let's first look at Jesus' humility. According to Matthew 11:29-30, Jesus told them, "Take my yoke upon you, and learn of me; for I am meek and lowly in heart: and ye shall find rest unto your souls. For my yoke *is* easy, and my burden is light."

This sentence is unique in the Gospel because Jesus, for the first time, calls attention to one of his characteristics: humility. He is not calling himself strong and courageous; he calls himself humble and meek. Why is that? Because in Jesus' mind, humility is the foremost Christian virtue. Not only that, but he also wanted to teach humility to his followers. In a sense, Jesus is saying to them: *"come to me. I want to teach you humility."*

In the popular culture of today's America, humility is not the right word. Indeed, humility has long been associated with being inferior to others, with a sense of imperfection and a willingness to submit to others. Today's dictionaries define humility as having a low self-regard, a sense of unworthiness, a low view of one's importance. However, in the context of the New Testament, none of these definitions apply, simply because Jesus doesn't meet them. Yet he calls himself meek and humble. Of all the virtues, Jesus places humility above all others.

Jesus gave his disciples three great lessons in humbleness: the example of the child (Matthews 18:4), the teachings on service (Matthews 25-28), and the case of washing feet (John 13). In choosing a child as the embodiment of humility, Jesus reminds us that a child is eager for learning, is docile, and is always curious. And free from vanity, ambitions, and social aspirations. In other words, Jesus would like us to be like children in the matter of faith, with open and sincere hearts. In John 13:16, when his disciples were filled with ambition and argued among themselves as to who should be the master in the kingdom of heaven, Jesus tells them: "Verily, verily, I say unto you, The servant is not greater than his lord; neither he that is sent greater than he that sent him." (John 13:16)

The third lesson in humility is given to his disciples on the very night of his betrayal after the Last Supper. The Gospel of John, chapter 13, describes how Jesus arises from the table, and taking a basin and girding Himself with a towel, proceeds to wash the dust from the disciples' feet. Here, again, we see what humility really is: It is laying down one's dignity, it is a willingness to come down, and it is a delight in rendering service. And why was it that Jesus was able to do this? Because he knew his godly origin and divine destiny, and he knew he was the Son of God.

This is, therefore, the secret of Christian humility and obedience: A man cannot be humble except by coming close to God. It is by thinking of the eternal that a mortal man becomes willing to do lowly things. Only a strong man can really be humble. St. Paul regards humility as the most divine grace he can find in Jesus: "And being found in fashion as a man, he humbled himself, and became obedient unto death, even the death of the cross." (Philippians 2:8)

REMEMBER: CHRISTIAN HUMILITY
CAN ONLY COME
FROM GOD

The Righteous Warrior

Now let's look at other attributes that Jesus the Righteous Warrior displayed during his first coming on the earth: strength, firmness, courage, and patience.

Jesus' Strength

What was the first impression that Jesus of Nazareth made upon his contemporaries? Was he perceived as insignificant and transitory, pale and ghastly, sickly and subdued, meek and weak? Of course not. On the contrary, the Gospels give us examples of Jesus acting as a leader, giving orders, dispatching people, and speaking with authority. In everything he does, he gives the impression of mastery, power, and leadership. His authority does not come from an earthly position of power because he holds none. His authority comes only from his inner strength and moral character. Jesus casts moral authority, the highest authority of all. He drew men to him. Only a man of strength attracts large masses of other men. Jesus was hated by many. Only a man of high strength makes his enemies hate and fear him.

But if Jesus made some men to hate him, he inspired many more to love him. He kindled a devotion that is superior to anything that has been ever known. He started a fire that ran all over Judea, then encircled the Mediterranean Sea, then spread into the German forests, and then jumped over the English Channel. Jesus' strength as a warrior was displayed in fighting the lonely fight, and taking all the blows his enemies directed at him. Indeed, he died on the battlefield by hanging on the cross, and in doing so, he won our salvation.

REMEMBER: JESUS' OUTWARD AUTHORITY
COMES FROM HIS HOLY INNER STRENGTH

Jesus' Firmness

When we think of Jesus, we usually think tenderness, gentleness, and graciousness. Yet, the kindness of nature cannot be considered virtue unless the tenacity of will accompanies it. Along with tenderness, there must be firmness, and underneath graciousness, there must lie a resolve as hard as steel. It is indeed only a strong character who dares run counter to the traditions and customs of the world in which he moves.

Yet when it comes to Jesus of Nazareth, we are in the presence of a man who nobody swerved or dominated. He was asked by his countrymen to lead them in the fight against the Roman occupation. Despite loving his homeland, Jesus refused. He did not take the advice of his family members when they were contrary to his mission. For this, his brothers resented him. Jesus resisted the temptation of the mighty forces of darkness for forty days when he was tested in the wilderness. *"Get thee behind me Satan"* was his final answer. An exemplary self-discipline accompanied Jesus' tenacity. When Jesus commits to going somewhere, he does it. When Jesus promises to cast out demons, he delivers.

It is in the firmness of Jesus that we find an indispensable element of Christian character. We Christians are to resist exterior forces and form our lives from within. We are not to be swayed by current opinions but guided only by the Holy Spirit. We are not to listen to voices of the time, but to live and work for eternity. In other words, Jesus shows us how to stay unchanged and unchangeable.

REMEMBER: JESUS' FIRMNESS COMES FROM HIS
LOVE, NOT FROM THE LOVE OF FIRMNESS

Jesus' Courage

Courage is a virtue that everybody admires. There has never been a nation that did not praise courageous men. Valor is one of the elemental qualities of the human spirit, one of the foundational stones in the magnificent structure of character, one of the shining virtues of man. There are different kinds of courage. There is a courage that we may call physical, which is an indifference to danger, a contempt for suffering and death. Then there is military courage, which is the most common in the world. There is also an occasional courage, that is born of some frenzied moment, such as the rescue of someone from fire or flood.

The courage displayed by Jesus was neither military nor occasional. It was the highest form of courage--the moral courage--which manifested itself in isolation and solitude. The audacity of Jesus of Nazareth was the courage of the quiet and commonplace days and nights. It was revealed hour by hour walking on dusty roads toward unknown destinations, preaching in front of large crowds.

When Jesus shows before Pontius Pilate, he stands so tall that Pilate is afraid of him. The heart of the Roman prefect fluttered when Jesus said to him, "Thou sayest that I am a king. To this end was I born, and for this cause came I into the world, that I should bear witness unto the truth. Every one that is of the truth heareth my voice." (John 18:37).

REMEMBER: JESUS DISPLAYED THE HIGHEST FORM
OF HUMAN COURAGE - THE MORAL COURAGE

Jesus' Patience

The word patience has two distinct meanings. The most common is "the calm waiting for something hoped for to take place." For instance, farmers patiently wait for spring to arrive. The second meaning is more brutal, being "the unruffled endurance to pain and suffering with no end in sight."[12]

Jesus waited patiently for thirty years before he began his ministry. He remained in the little country town of Galilee before he entered into the labors he felt God had given him to do. We do not ask ourselves how much this must have troubled him. Could he have started his work when he was eighteen, or twenty or twenty-five? Of course, he could have. He was patiently waiting to discover the plans his Father had for him, until one day when he received them. He was thirty.

When his tribulations began on the night of his betrayal in the Garden of Gethsemane, Jesus first refused to defend himself in the court of law offered by the Romans, then accepted his sentencing with serenity. For several days and nights, he endured indignities at the hands of his tormentors. Then Jesus suffered with patience and resignation, the most horrific pain that can be inflicted on the human body. After two thousand years since his death on the cross, Jesus is still patiently waiting for the human heart to surrender and accept the truth he proclaimed. And yet he will most likely give us another day, and still another, saying: *Perhaps tomorrow the sin will be repented.*

> ## REMEMBER: JESUS ENDURED HIS TRIBULATIONS WITH DIVINE PATIENCE

What have we learned from examining the character of Jesus Christ, the Man? Perhaps the takeaway is that developing a Christlike character should be the ultimate goal of all believers. Why is that? Because as Pastor Warren tells us, *"God intends to make you like Jesus."*[13] To settle for anything less is to miss the point of our lives. Building the character of Christ is life's most important task because the way we live is all about our growing into him. This means that the objective of Christian teaching must be to change lives, not merely provide information.

Teaching a Christlike character should start in the family, continue in school, and then become a lifelong self-development goal of each individual. This is because integrity is never built in a classroom or during a single study course. Character is built slowly, deliberately, and over a long time in the circumstances of real life. Bible study classes are great for identifying character qualities and learn how to develop a character. Small groups are great for helping each other hone the characteristics God is growing in us. But character is formed only in the difficult circumstances of life. When we understand this, we will be able to respond correctly when God places us in character-building opportunities.

Moments of Reflection

1. Why should we study Jesus' character?
2. List some of Jesus' traits of character presented in the Gospels.
3. What does Preacher C. E. Jefferson reveal about Jesus' authority as a leader?

4. What is humility?

5. Where does Jesus' moral authority come from?

6. Provide examples of Jesus' firmness and tenacity of will.

7. What is moral courage?

8. Which are the two meanings of patience? Why is patience necessary?

9. Why is developing a Christlike character so important to believers?

10. What does it take to build one's character?

YOU ARE A CHRISTIAN

—◆•◆•◆—

Virtues: Faith, Hope, Love

"For God so loved the world, that he gave his only begotten Son, that whosoever believeth in him should not perish, but have everlasting life." (John 3:16)

CHAPTER 3
YOUR CHRISTIAN LIFE

———◆·◆·●·◆·◆———

"And ye shall know the truth, and the truth
shall make you free." (John 8:32)

I must have been about seven years old when I asked my grandfather, *"Grandpa, what should I do to be a good Christian like you?"* At that time, my grandfather was an ordained priest at the Orthodox Church in Sebes, a small town in Transylvania where I was born. My parents and I were living in another city, but we were visiting relatives in Sebes every summer. Almost every Sunday, I would go with my cousins to attend the liturgy performed by my Grandpa, and I was impressed by the majestic rituals, his loud voice, and the smell of incense in the church. In response to my question, my Grandpa said, *"Grandson, you already are a Christian because I baptized you in Christ shortly after you were born. But now, as a boy, you must fully receive Jesus in your heart and follow his commands. If you do so, He will be there to counsel and protect you when you are in trouble, when you are sick or simply want to talk to Him".*

And so I did for the rest of my life.

Stepping Stone 1 is the platform on which we review what it means to live a life in Christ. We all have our personal story on how and why we became believers, and perhaps this is the most famous story of our life. Yet not too many of us live our lives following Christian teachings. In this chapter, we'll look at our duties as Christians: what's the significance of a "purpose-driven life," what it means to "be like Jesus," and "walk like Jesus."

Stepping Stone 1 represents the great Christian virtues of Faith, Hope, and Love.

Who is a Christian?

The best definition comes from the Bible itself: " Be ye followers of me, even as I also *am* of Christ." (1 Corinthians 11:1)

What Peter is saying here is that a true Christian is someone who keeps Jesus' commandments and walks like Jesus. In other words, a true Christian must meet two criteria: (i) to confess to be a Christian, and (ii) to conduct his life as a Christian.

Confession of faith: this is the first condition to be called a Christian, that of professing to the world that you have accepted Jesus Christ as your Lord and Savior.

Walking like Jesus did: this is the second condition to be called a Christian, and perhaps the more difficult one. It is also called Christlikeness, or to be like Christ. To start with, it requires not only a thorough understanding of Jesus' life and work during his ministry on earth two millennia ago, but also a study of his character as a man.

A Purpose-Driven Life

How should we live our lives as Christians? How should we apply the great Scriptural teachings to our way of thinking, speaking, and behaving? In answering these questions, we will be using the concept of A Purpose-Driven Life introduced by Pastor Rick Warren in his influential book with the same title published in 2002.[14]

The major points made by Pastor Warren are that your life is not an accident, and its purpose is not about you. It is about God. Your life has a primary mission that was established by God long before you or your parents were born. You find God's purpose for you only by talking to God. Once you know your purpose, your life will get deep meaning; it will get simplified and have a focus point.

A purpose-driven life is, therefore, an experience guided, controlled, and protected by God. And what does God demand in return? He expects to be recognized, praised, and glorified as your Lord. There are many ways to bring glory to God, but the important ones are embedded in God's five purposes for your life.

Purpose Number 1: Worshipping God

Anything you do to bring pleasure to God is an act of worship. When you attend church, Mass, or listen to a sermon; when you pray or sing with fellow believers; when you light a candle in the memory of your parents; when you communicate with the Lord in seclusion, you worship God. This kind of worship is essential, but it is not enough. Praising God should be a lifestyle. Every activity can be transformed into an act of worship when you do it for the pleasure, glory, and praise of the Almighty.

Purpose Number 2: Loving Others

The entire Bible is about God's love for his people and him building a family who will love him, honor him, and reign with him forever. You were formed to be part of God's family. When you place your faith in Christ, God becomes your Father. You become his child, other believers become your brothers and sisters, and the church becomes your spiritual family.

How to love is the most important lesson God wants you to learn on earth. The love you need to learn is not the worldly self-centered love. It is the godly unselfish love that emanates only from Jesus Christ. This kind of love is not only benevolent; it is also surrendering, sacrificial, and eternal.

" A new commandment I give unto you, That ye love one another; as I have loved you, that ye also love one another." (John 13:34)

Purpose Number 3: Becoming like Christ

From the very beginning, God has planned to make you like His Son. Becoming like Christ means taking on his character, values, and attitudes. It is the Holy Spirit's job to produce Christlike character in you. You cannot reproduce the character of Jesus on your strength alone.

It follows that Christlikeness is not provided by imitation, but by inhabitation, by allowing the Holy Spirit to dwell in us. With the Holy Spirit inside us, we must always consult with him before making decisions. If we choose the right thing, God's spirit will give us his power, faith, and wisdom to do it. This is how you cooperate with the Holy Spirit; this is how your character develops. Apostle Paul outlines in Ephesians 4:22 the three things we must do in becoming like Jesus: (i) choose to let go of old ways of acting, (ii) change the way we think, and lastly (iii) put on the character of Christ by developing new, godly habits. Your character is essentially the sum of your patterns of thinking, speaking, and acting. When we build our character, we primarily grow up spiritually. And this is precisely what God wants of us.

We are transformed by the Truth, by trouble, and by temptation. Spiritual growth is the process of replacing lies with the Truth by reading and absorbing the Word of God. God uses life circumstances, particularly hardship, to develop our character; therefore, everything that happens to us has spiritual significance. Similarly, every temptation is an opportunity to grow and do good. There are no shortcuts to spiritual maturity. The development of Christlike character takes time, perseverance, and effort. Similar to physical growth, spiritual growth toward maturation cannot be rushed. Christlikeness is your eventual destination, but the journey will last a lifetime.

Purpose Number 4: Serving Others

You were put on earth to make a contribution, to add something to the life on earth, not just to take from it. God wants you to give something back. This is called ministry or service, and it is God's fourth purpose for your life. Doing ministry is your duty toward fellow Christians; it is your obligation toward the Body of Christ. This is your assignment that you must fulfill cheerfully, regularly, and to the best of your abilities. Don't be concerned that you may not be adequate for the job. God loves being served by all people, including inadequate, weak, or meek people. The Bible is filled with examples of how God loves using imperfect, ordinary people to do extraordinary things despite their weaknesses.

Purpose Number 5: Telling Others About God

You were made for a mission. God is at work in the world, and he wants you to join him. This assignment is called your mission. Besides your ministry within the Body of Christ, God wants you to have a task in the world to serve the unbelievers. "For so hath the Lord commanded us, *saying*, I have set thee to be a light of the Gentiles, that thou shouldest be for salvation unto the ends of the earth." (Acts 13:47)

The mission Jesus had while on earth is now our mission because we are the Body of Christ. What he did in his physical body, we are to continue as his spiritual body, his church. What is that mission? Introducing people to God! Telling them the Good News! Helping them to come to Christ! Therefore, fulfilling your mission on earth is an essential part of living for God's glory.

> REMEMBER: YOUR FIVE PURPOSES IN LIFE ARE OF DIVINE CALLING. THEY MUST BE ACCOMPLISHED WITH PASSION, PERSEVERANCE AND HUMILITY

Walking in Jesus' Footsteps

To most Christians, walking in Jesus' footsteps should mean two things: building a character like his, and serving like Jesus. Every Christian man or woman should aspire to be like Jesus and be capable of living a life which mirrors Jesus' teachings. Why is that? Because we are called to do it, because it should be our passion, and because it is our destiny. This task will indeed require above-average dedication, perseverance, and patience, but it can be done. Then there is the question of why: Why should you become like Jesus?

The answer comes straight from the Bible: " For whom he did foreknow, he also did predestinate *to be* conformed to the image of his Son, that he might be the firstborn among many brethren." (Romans 8:29)

Building a Character like Jesus

Building a Christlike character - which I call Diamond Soul - is the result of the most profound process of personal change. From a biblical perspective, this miraculous metamorphosis takes place this way. In the first phase, as we let the Holy Spirit indwelling in us, we absorb his teachings and allow him to act upon us. Thus, we receive the truth and become transformed by it. Then slowly, as the Christlike character inside us grows more robust, the Holy Spirit teachings begin emanating from us like radiating rays. This is the phase during which we release the truth, thus creating the climate for transforming others.

> **O worship the LORD**
> **in the beauty of holiness:**
> **fear before him, all the earth.**
> **Psalm 96:9**

When contemplating crafting a Diamond Soul character, the question arises: which character traits evident in Jesus' character should you focus on? There are so many! Scholars have identified twenty-two attributes of Jesus' character.[15] They are divine and perfect because Jesus was divine and perfect. We mortals cannot possibly expect to become like him. But we should be able to emulate a few of these attributes, which will match well our temperament and begin incorporating them into our new character.

My own choice has been to put humility at the center of my Christ-like character. I did this because I consider humility the essential Christian virtue, and it matches my temperament well. Besides this, I selected four attributes that made Jesus the Righteous Warrior during his time on earth: strength, firmness, courage, and patience. These, too, I find fit well with my aspirations.

Building a Diamond Soul character will mature you spiritually and transform you into a humble, productive, and joyful servant of God. It will put you on the wondrous path of discovering your full personal potential and growing into the person the Almighty wants you to be. Diamond Soul goals and processes can be regarded as a Bible-based, sequential, and well-integrated personal development training program. Follow it, and you will benefit greatly.

As you start crafting your Christlike character, keep this fundamental truth in mind: You cannot do it alone, the Holy Spirit must guide you. The Bible tells us that the Holy Spirit does the heavy lifting, but you must enthusiastically cooperate with him. Character building is a collaborative process between the Holy Spirit and you. Your new character includes all the Fruits of the Spirit, but also derivative values easily understood and appreciated by the mortal world.

Elsewhere in this material, I have likened the Diamond Soul character with a natural diamond. Both are beautiful, durable, and precious. The significant difference, however, is this: the real diamond is a material object without life; the Diamond Soul character is a living entity providing the gift of life through the Holy Spirit.

REMEMBER: YOUR DIAMOND SOUL CHARACTER CAN ONLY BE BUILT UNDER THE GUIDANCE OF THE HOLY SPIRIT AND WITH YOUR HARD WORK

Acting like Jesus

Ministry is what Christians are called to do to serve the Body of Christ. At its core, the ministry is about applying Christ's principles into our daily lives when dealing with fellow believers. We should worship with them, support them and cooperate with them. Here are some practical examples of what you can do daily:

- In the family: create and maintain an atmosphere of love, sincerity, and support; spend quality one-on-one time with spouse, children, and close friends regularly; give thanks before each meal with your family; reserve time for devotion and prayer every day.
- At church: attend church regularly; volunteer your time to fulfill the church's needs; participate at fellowship activities; support your church financially.
- In the neighborhood and at work: be an example of Christian character and ethical conduct.

> REMEMBER: YOUR MINISTRY IS TO SERVE
> FELLOW CHRISTIANS

Mission is what we are called to do as we mingle with the unbelieving world. At its core, the task is about applying Christ's principles into our daily lives when dealing with unbelievers. We should befriend them, we should cooperate with them, and we should share the Good News with them. Following are some practical examples of what you can do daily:

- In the family, assuming you have members of your direct or extended family who have not received Jesus Christ: create and maintain an atmosphere of love, openness, and support; do not discriminate in any way against unbelievers; give thanks before each meal; spend quality one-on-one time with all members of your family.

- In the neighborhood: be an example of Christian character, faith, and behavior; socialize regularly with your all neighbors; do not discriminate; be sensitive to their needs and offer help; initiate activities to improve the quality of life in the neighborhood;

- At work: be an example of ethical conduct; be courteous, polite, and helpful to everyone; if in a leadership position, correspondingly treat believers and unbelievers; become a servant leader by using your moral authority; when necessary, defend the faith in a smart, courteous yet firm way.

- If on an evangelizing mission out of town: establish trust by befriending and helping first; only then bring up faith in a way that is suitable to the unbeliever; discuss issues of faith in a piece-by-piece fashion; do not overwhelm your interlocutor. You know that your efforts bear fruits when the unbeliever comes to you to ask questions about the faith.

> REMEMBER: YOUR MISSION IS
> TO SERVE, INFLUENCE
> AND CONVERT FELLOW UNBELIEVERS

Standing on Stepping Stone 1

As you have reached the first stepping stone on your journey toward the summit, you can rest a bit and take stock of what has happened to you so far:

You have a better sense of the purpose of your Christian life on this earth.

You have learned what it takes to craft the new Christ-like Diamond Soul character.

For these reasons, Stepping Stone 1 becomes the spiritual foundation of the new character you are constructing. Standing on it now, you can set your eyes with confidence on the next target of the climb - Stepping Stone 2. This is what we will be talking about in the next chapter. And if you think you know who you are, be prepared for some shockers!

REMEMBER: CHRISTIAN FAITH IS THE
SPIRITUAL FOUNDATION OF YOUR
DIAMOND SOUL CHARACTER

Moments of Reflection

1. How have you done so far regarding your five purposes in life?

2. What Christ's trait of character would you put at the center of your new Diamond Soul character? Why?

3. How are you planning to build your Diamond Soul character? When are you going to start?

4. Since faith is the spiritual foundation of your Diamond Soul character, what are you doing to strengthen it?

YOU ARE A FIGHTER

—◆•◆•◆—

Virtues: Prudence, Responsibility, Courage

"I can do all things through Christ which
strengtheneth me." (Philippians 4:13)

CHAPTER 4
WHO ARE YOU?

———◆·◆·◆———

"And the LORD God formed man *of* the dust of the ground, and breathed into his nostrils the breath of life; and man became a living soul." (Genesis 2:7)

My best friend Juju and I used to walk in the public park and then go to a beer garden almost every Friday after school or work. We were teenagers who enjoyed life, loved to discover new things, and were endowed with curious minds. One evening, perhaps after one too many beers, I asked him, *"Juju, can you tell me who we are? Are we really descendants of monkeys as they teach us in school? Or are we something else? And why are we on this earth? Who put us here?"* Wow, I was astonished at the words coming out of my mouth! That was the first time I uttered them, perhaps the result of some thoughts deep inside my brain. My best friend was even more astonished than I was because he did not expect our teenage conversation to take such a turn. He said, *"George, I have no idea of what you're talking about. I think we are on this earth because our mothers gave birth to us here, that's all. Regarding the monkey business, I can tell you for sure that I am not a monkey!"* After chatting a bit longer, we went to each other's homes. But those questions had haunted me for many years, even perhaps for the rest of my life.

Stepping Stone 2 is the platform on which you will learn about the principles of proactivity applied to the way you think, speak, and behave. It represents the Christian virtues of Prudence, Responsibility, and Courage. Proactivity is the ability to control situations by causing something to happen rather than responding to it after it has happened. Proactivity means inquiring about oneself, finding out who we truly are, and resolving to improve ourselves continuously.

Stepping Stone 2 is also called the platform of Personal Vision because it gives us an overall understanding of who actually lives inside my body. It is the image we have in our heads about our persona. It is how we see ourselves with our Creator and our fellow men. Building Personal Vision starts with the process of examination called introspection and ends up with a deep comprehension of ourselves called self-knowledge.

In this chapter, we will learn about introspection and self-knowledge, the four dimensions of human life, and why we are the way we are.

Personal Vision

Let's first have a brief look at the concepts of introspection and self-knowledge.

Introspection

As children of God created in his image, we humans are endowed with the faculty of self-awareness. Self-awareness is how a person consciously knows and understands his/her character, feelings, motives, and desires. Self-awareness is the ability to recognize oneself as a separate entity from the surroundings and other individuals. Introspection, on the other hand, is the deliberate examination of one's conscious thoughts and feelings.

**Knowing yourself is
the beginning of all wisdom
Aristotle**

Introspection makes us ask questions like "Who am I?" "What constitutes the true me?" and "Why am I the way I am?" Such inquiries are as old as humanity. They have been asked from times immemorial by philosophers belonging to all civilizations, cultures, and religions. For instance, the Greek philosopher Plato (428-348 BC) asked, *"...why should we not calmly and patiently review our thoughts, and thoroughly examine what these appearances in us really are?"*[16] From a Christian perspective, introspection is searching for, finding, and establishing a connection with the Holy Spirit that dwells inside us. Once this connection is established, it becomes the link between God and us.

Self-Knowledge

The answers given to the questions raised by introspection make up the body of information called self-knowledge or self-concept. One's self-knowledge is a collection of beliefs about oneself. It consists of the total of emotions, ideas, desires, fears, rational thoughts, and traits of character that define our true self.[17] It stands to reason that each of us will gain trough introspection the self-knowledge distinct and specific to each individual. Therefore, we can safely say that self-knowledge includes our peculiar way of looking at ourselves and the world around us. How we regard ourselves is called mentality, and it is vastly different from one individual to another, from our culture to another. Why does this matter? Simply because mentality makes us think, speak, and behave in a certain way. In a sense, we, as persons, are the fruit of our mindset.

> REMEMBER: SELF-KNOWLEDGE IS ACHIEVED
> THROUGH INTROSPECTION UNDER THE
> GUIDANCE OF THE HOY SPIRIT

Being Human

So, who are we, humans? What does it mean to be human? To answer this question, we must go way back in time to the dawn of our Christian roots. We believe we are descendants of Adam and Eve, the first man and woman created by God in his image. From the very beginning, the Almighty told them to multiply, and gave their children the right to take dominion of the earth. When God created Adam, he gave him a body made of the dust of the earth and then breathed life into him, thus giving him a Spirit and a Soul. God also made Eve from a rib of Adam's body, to be Adam's companion.

Christian teachings tell us that man has three parts: body, soul, and spirit, to reflect the triune nature of God himself, i.e., Father, Son, and Holy Spirit. The body (flesh) is the material part of the man which can be seen and touched. It is temporal. The soul and spirit are the immaterial parts of man, which are intangibles. They include emotions, intellect, mind, conscience, and so forth, which make up the soul and spirit of man. They are eternal.

For this book, I decided to group the intangibles in a slightly different manner to align better with our 21st-century knowledge of man. From this viewpoint, we humans have a material body, intellect (mind), emotions, and a spirit. This view is supported by our findings when we look at ourselves: we see our bodies, we are aware of our intellect, we feel our emotions, and we sense our spirituality. We will call these the four dimensions of the human nature.

The First Dimension: Physical

We now know that the human body is nothing but a miraculous, vastly complex, and extremely complicated electro-biochemical machinery. The human body is the most astonishing and marvelous living organism studied by science. It is incredible how from just a few chemical elements found in nature, such complexity could emerge. About seventy-five percent of our body is made of water, (which in its turn is made of two atoms of hydrogen and one of oxygen), eighteen percent is carbon, and three percent is nitrogen. The remaining four percent consists of other elements such as calcium, sulfur, magnesium, and iron, which are essential for sustaining life.[18] Atoms combine into complex organic molecules, which in turn become biological cells that display the marvelous cycle of life: birth, growth, reproduction, and death.

Living cells grow and multiply in accordance with specific rules found in their genetic code to form tissues and organs, which together make the human body. Recent research shows that most bio-cells in the body renew themselves every seven years. In other words, we get a new body every seven years! Our bodies provide the physical and biochemical support on which the other three assets of ours––intellect, emotions, and spirit––exist. "What? know ye not that your body is the temple of the Holy Ghost *which is* in you, which ye have of God, and ye are not your own?" (Corinthians 6:19)

The Second Dimension: Mental/Intellectual

The second dimension defines the ability of humans to think, speak, and write. The seat of this fantastic faculty is the brain, another marvel of the divine creation. The brain is the central organ of the nervous system. It controls most of the activities of the body, processing, integrating, and coordinating the information received from sensing organs, while sending commands to actuating organs. The brain also performs other complex cognitive processes such as abstract thinking, decision making, behavior, memory storage, speech, and language. At the highest level, there are four more unique characteristics of us humans: self-awareness, conscience, imagination and will-power.[19]

Brain activity is made possible by the interconnections of specialized cells called neurons. The number of neurons in the adult brain is believed to be close to eighty-six billion, which is about half the number of stars contained in the Milky Way galaxy.[20] A neuron consists of a cell body, axon, and dendrites. Dendrites are branches that receive information from the dendrites of other neurons. The place where two dendrites meet is called a synapse. The signals received and transmitted through synapse are of a highly complex electro-chemical nature, and their intimate working is still not well understood.

In the last analysis, the billions of synapses in the brain make an unbelievable vast network of possible pathways for information to flow and store. Even though most synapses are made in the first months of a baby's life, scientists now agree that new synapses are also continually made through learning during one's whole life. This phenomenon is called neuroplasticity.[21] The implications of this relatively recent discovery are enormous: It means that if disease or old age destroys existing neuronal links, information may still flow on new synapse pathways. This fact provides the scientific foundation for the following assertion: what humans have learned can be unlearned, and then replaced by new learning. In other words, bad old habits of thinking, speaking, and acting can be replaced by good new ones!

The Third Dimension: Emotions

The third dimension covers the emotional aspects of human life. The dictionary defines emotion as "a natural instinctive state of mind deriving from one's circumstances, mood, or relationships with others."[22] Thus, emotions are instinctive or intuitive feelings as distinguished from reasoning or knowledge. They include joy, sorrow, fear, love, hate, etc. In this material, the terms emotions and feelings are used interchangeably.

The study of emotions and feelings belongs to the field of psychology. Psychology concerns itself with all aspects of behavior and mental processes. It includes topics such as how the brain works, how our memory is organized, how people interact in groups, and how children learn about the world. Significant contributions to the modern field of psychoanalysis were brought by the Austrian neurologist Sigmund Freud (1856 - 1939). Freud's theory on human mental life includes three distinct, interacting agents called ID (instincts), EGO (realism), and SUPER-EGO (consciousness).[23] Freud is also the father of the "theory of determinism," which asserts that people are predetermined by their heritage, upbringing, and personal experiences––and nothing can be done to change that. Fortunately, life has proved this theory wrong, as we shall see later on.

Emotions can be powerful neurological storms in our central nervous system. They may change from day to day, apparently for no reason, taking us on a hard-to-control emotional roller coaster. They are, therefore, mighty forces in human behavior. For this material, we will consider the heart to be the seat of feelings and emotions, this metaphor being in line with the famous saying, "I love you from the bottom of my heart." From a Christian perspective, we can say that all positive emotions such as love, optimism, compassion, and care are manifestations of God on earth. In contrast, negative emotions like hate, envy, cruelty, and anger are the source of evil in life.

The Fourth Dimension: Spirituality

Spirituality is the fourth dimension of human nature, and the most controversial from a scientific perspective. Spirituality is as old as humanity, yet it is least understood. According to Webster's Dictionary, spirituality is "the quality of being concerned with the human spirit or soul as opposed to material or physical things."[24] Related to it, there are two more terms to be mentioned: faith and religion. Faith is the belief in a divine authority, while religion is the set of teachings, dogmas, and practices supporting faith. Since secular science has traditionally studied mostly the material world, spirituality has not been one of its concerns, even though most people on earth embrace some form of it. Fortunately for humankind, during the last several millennia, great minds have searched for answers regarding faith, trying to gain knowledge about it. "Now faith is the substance of things hoped for, the evidence of things not seen." (Hebrews 11:1) For us, believers in Jesus Christ, faith is the foundation of our lives, and the Holy Spirit represents our spirituality.

> REMEMBER: GOD HAS ENDOWED US WITH BODY, INTELLECT, EMOTIONS AND THE HOLY SPIRIT

So, Who are You?

As Christians of the twenty-first century, we believe that the material and spiritual worlds, although fundamentally different from each other, are compatible with each other. We should not regard them as opposite and exclusionary, but rather complementing and supporting each other. Both of them define who we are, and both of them should help us become better people. In other words, faith, reason, religion, and science can and should harmoniously coexist in each of us. Starting from these premises, let's attempt to answer the question of "Who are You?" as follows:

You are a child of God, a unique and distinct individual created by Almighty in his image. Your human nature reflects some of God's attributes, although in a limited way. Because you have accepted Jesus Christ as your Lord and Savior, the Holy Spirit is within you. You want to be compassionate, faithful, truthful, kind, patient, and just. However, these divine qualities may have been distorted by the original sin, which also resides in you.

You live in the physical body that God gave you. The Scriptures teach us to regard the body as the temple in which the Holy Spirit resides. You must take good care of it. To maintain the health and vigor of the body, you eat balanced nutrition, exercise every day, and get proper rest and sleep. You refrain from using harmful substances that may be detrimental to the wellbeing of the body, or from adopting unhealthy lifestyles.

You are an intelligent human being, endowed by Creator with the ability to think, speak, and write. You use intellectual curiosity to gain an understanding of Him and his vast and intricate designs, as much as he allows you to do so. You also use your mind to think through new ways to better yourself, to improve the life of your family, and to be of service to others. You pay special attention to issues of morality and ethics because they are vitally important to a healthy and prosperous society.

Your emotions and feelings are an integral part of how God made you. You understand that emotions and feelings are mighty forces in your own life, as well as in your interactions with others. For these reasons, you focus on positive and uplifting emotions such as joy, gratitude, serenity, hope, pride, awe, amusement, inspiration, and love. When detecting negative feelings in your heart, such as worry, stress, hate, anger, sadness, and so on, you play them down or attempt corrective actions. You are also fully aware that your willpower can mitigate negative emotions and feelings.

Your faith in God is the center of your spirituality. You know that the Holy Spirit resides in you, in your whole being. It gives you strength to go through the daily challenges of life and guides the journey on this earth. Your faith is the intimate, profound, and deeply personal relationship that you have with Jesus Christ, your Lord. You know that faith is your only immovable anchor during stormy times, and a reservoir of resilience during recovery. It is also the primary source of energizing joy and elation in your life.

In closure, to our humanistic friends who may have a hard time accepting that humans are God's children, let's offer them a new definition of man using an evolutionist phrase they surely understand. We all know that the current scientific term for the human race is 'homo sapiens,' which means 'intelligent man.' Let's say we propose to enhance this definition by making one modification to it: let's attach the adjective 'spiritual'. So, dear humanistic friends, you can consider all my fellow believers and me as 'Homo Sapiens Spiritualis.' We trust this is a definition you can live with! We also propose that the public schools should teach students that the human race should be called 'Homo Sapiens Spiritualis'!

> REMEMBER: YOU ARE A CHILD OF GOD
> ENDOWED WITH BODY, INTELLECT,
> EMOTIONS AND HOLY SPIRIT

Why are You this Way?

From a Christian perspective, you are the way you are because of your generational blessings and curses. Generational blessings are those which flow from father to son. So are generational curses that sons receive from their fathers. Your generational benefits include the First Covenant that God made with Abraham and his successors: "And I will establish my covenant between me and thee and thy seed after thee in their generations for an everlasting covenant, to be a God unto thee, and to thy seed after thee." (Genesis 17:7-8)

You must honor the generations that came before you by recognizing and walking in the teachings they have passed on to you. As your father has blessed you, so will you consecrate your sons. At the same time, you must be fully aware of the tremendous generational curse caused by Adam and Eve, your very first parents, when they transgressed God's commandment and were expelled from the Garden of Eden. Also, the sins of your ancestors were passed down to their descendants, including you, as the Bible teaches: "for I the LORD thy God *am* a jealous God, visiting the iniquity of the fathers upon the children unto the third and fourth *generation* of them that hate me;" (Genesis 34:7). Therefore, be aware that you will also transmit sins to your children's children according to the same biblical law.

Now let's try to use scientific language to answer the question: "*Why are you the way you are?*" The short answer is, due to chance and choice. Chance is made up of your ancestors' genes and your childhood environment. It defines most of who you are today. Heredity and upbringing are unique and specific to each individual. On the other hand, choice consists of decisions others made for you as a child, and by selections you made yourself later on as a teenager and young adult. Similarly, choice in life is unique and specific to each of us.

The dominant theory of human development in the last two hundred years or so has been "determinism." It asserts that the specific genes of each individual determine human behavior, beliefs, and desires. Determinism says that we are the product of heredity, our own experiences, and the environment, and there's nothing we can do about it. Austrian neurologist Sigmund Freud (1856-1939) is considered the father of determinism. He looked at the man through the eyes of a researcher, and found it to be a restricted living being, not a creation of God with unlimited potential. The significant negative consequence of believing in determinism is that it is a self-fulfilling prophecy. It makes you a slave of your past and negates your ability to change yourself in the present or the future.

When teaching about human nature and determinism, Dr. Steven R. Covey (1932-2012) liked to split determinism in three parts: genetic, physical, and environmental.[25] Paraphrasing his words, this is what he used to say in his distinctive humorous way:

Genetic determinism: "Your grandparents did it to you. That's why you have such a short temper. Your grandpa had a short fuse, and it's now in your DNA. It just goes through the generations, and you have inherited it."

Physical determinism: "Your parents did it to you. It's the way they brought you up, the way they talked to you, or how they punished you. That's why you are so shy and incapable of standing up before a group of people. It's all their fault!"

Environmental determinism: "Your school did it to you. It did not teach you anything of value; all teachers were useless. Besides, those bullies in the schoolyard used to terrorize and beat you up. It is not your failing that even now, so many years after, you are afraid of people and cannot stare anyone in his eyes. It cannot be your fault; it must be theirs!"

Fortunately for us, Austrian psychiatrist and Holocaust survivor Viktor E. Frankl (1905-1997) challenged Freud's theory of determinism at both theoretical and practical levels. In his seminal book *Man's Search for Meaning*,[26] Frankl argues that we cannot avoid suffering, but we can choose how to cope with it, find meaning in it, and move forward. He also asserts that the primary human drive is not pleasure or pain, but the pursuit of what we consider meaningful. Frankl shows that having a purpose in life is the most compelling transformative force. With it, man can fight back against the chains of his heredity and upbringing, and win. Thus, Frankl gave birth to the concept of proactivity, which will be the object of discussion of the following chapter.

It is worth mentioning that recent studies in epigenetics[27] strongly support Frankl's view that man's behavior patterns can be changed positively. They also reveal that our life experiences and choices do change us, including our brains, down to the DNA level. And these changes can be passed onto our children and further down along the hereditary line. Thus, the biblical concept of generational benefits or curses is fully confirmed by science.

> REMEMBER: YOU CAN FIGHT AGAINST
> HEREDITARY AND UPBRINGING CHAINS
> OF YOUR PAST BY FINDING A
> MEANINGFUL PURPOSE IN LIFE

Now, since you started to understand who you are at this point in time, let's explore how you can become the better person you aspire to be in the future. Do you know who you want to be five years from now? Do you know how to define that new person? And do you know how to get there? Find the unexpected answers in the next chapter!

Moments of Reflection

1. Take several days during which you inquire about yourself in tranquility. What do you find? Do you like what you see?
2. How are the four dimensions of life inter-related to each other? Which one is most important in your case?
3. Does the proposed new secular definition of the human race as "Homo Sapiens Spiritualis" make sense to you? Could you defend it in an intellectual debate with fellow unbelievers?

CHAPTER 5
PROACTIVE AND REACTIVE PEOPLE

I n 1994, I was attending a conference for executive self-development in one of the big cities on the West Coast. One of the keynote speakers was Dr. Steven R. Covey, a well-respected specialist in the field.[28] A few months earlier, I had listened to one of his audiotapes in which he was talking about two behavior patterns: proactive and reactive. I was utterly confused about those terms. I could not grasp their deeper meaning, so I decided to further pursue the matter by registering for that conference. As Dr. Covey stepped on the stage and started talking about proactivity and reactivity, I had a Eureka moment: *"Aha, being proactive means being in charge, and being reactive means being driven by others!"* From that instant, I realized that my very nature was proactive, but I still had to work much to improve myself. I also gathered that most of the people around me were of a reactive makeup. For this reason, I committed myself to helping those people to cross into the "being in charge" camp.

How Can Change Happen?

In the previous chapter, we learned how Viktor Frankl rejected Freud's concept of determinism based on heredity and upbringing environment. Frankl used the word proactive to describe a person who took responsibility for his or her life rather than looking for excuses in outside circumstances or blaming other people.

Frankl promoted the idea that if a man finds a purpose in life, he can transform himself by breaking the emotional chains of his past. The remaining question for him was how to break those chains practically and irreversibly. To this end, Frankl studied the reactive model of behavior, the instinctive bio-mechanism by which the human body responds to changes coming from outside. For instance, if a bright light hits our eyes, our natural bio-mechanism closes the eyelids without us even thinking about it. Such responses are called instinctive reactions. They are very fast and out of the control of the rational mind. Frankl's great insight made him observe that people react the same way when they think, speak, or behave with others. For instance, when someone raises the voice at us, we tend to respond by raising our voice, too. Or, when someone insults us, we tend to offend in response.

To change that, Frankl proposed a dramatic two-step change to the reactive response:

1. Introduce a several-seconds delay before you reply.
2. Base your reply on something you value, not on the emotions of the moment.

Thus, he gave birth to the "proactive model": when a stimulus is received, control your impulse to answer right back, take a few seconds to think, and respond by your values based on principles. Let's call such a response a "considerate response."

We believers surely are familiar with this model because it was stated two millennia earlier by Jesus Christ, and it has since been at the foundation of our Christian faith. This is how Jesus exemplified a proactive response based on Christian values, "And unto him that smiteth thee on the *one* cheek offer also the other; and him that taketh away thy cloke forbid not *to take thy* coat also." (Luke 6:29)

Modifying your behavior from a reactive to a proactive model is the only way to bring change into your life. There is no other path to self-transformation but proactivity. Only proactivity can give birth to a new you and free you from the emotional chains of the past. However, adopting proactivity is not easy to do. It takes willpower, know-how, practice, and patience. And above all, it will require faith in the divine guidance and help of the Holy Spirit. But once you master it, and have internalized it, it will become your new nature, and the proactive model will work miracles for you.

> REMEMBER: ADOPTING THE PROACTIVE
> MODEL WILL LIBERATE YOU FROM THE
> SHACKLES OF YOUR OWN PAST!

Two Types of Behavior Patterns

Sociologists tell us that society is composed of people whose behavior patterns broadly fall into two categories: reactive and proactive. According to Pareto's law of unequal distribution, reactive people probably make up 80 percent of the population, while proactive people count for the other 20 percent.[29] I fathom that the same Pareto 80/20 law should apply to the distribution of reactive and proactive behavior patterns in each individual: about 80 percent reactive and only 20 percent proactive. This chapter will show how to transform most of the reactive habits into proactive ones, thus trending toward the perfect goal of being 100 percent proactive.

How do we determine if people are reactive or proactive? By observing their behavior patterns in thinking, speaking, and acting. The table below contrasts the two:

REACTIVE PEOPLE	PROACTIVE PEOPLE
Cynical, pessimistic	Optimistic
Life is a struggle.	Life is a blessing.
Feel victimized	Feel in charge
Low self-image and self-esteem	Positive self-image, high self-esteem
Blame others and circumstances	Blame no one
Do not admit mistakes	Apologize after mistakes
Are critical of others	Are compassionate to others
Are suspicious of others	Put trust in others
Cannot control your own emotions	Can control own emotions
Are dependent on others	Are independent

Reactive people are affected emotionally by others around them. When they are treated well, they feel well; when not, they become sad, defensive, or protective. Reactive people build their emotional lives around the behavior of others. Thus, a reactive person becomes a slave to other's emotions. In contrast, a proactive person is a master of his emotions. Dynamic people are still affected by external stimuli, whether physical, social, or psychological. But their response to them is value-based. Proactive people are value-driven, not emotion-driven. Reactive behavior denotes weakness, bondage, and low self-worth. Proactive conduct projects leadership, freedom, and dignity.

We all display pieces of reactive and proactive behavior in a mixed manner. The challenge is to embrace more and more the dynamic model until it becomes an internalized habit--and thus, our new nature. Do not expect it to happen overnight. Recent studies show that internalizing a new habit takes at least two months of continuous and conscious practice.[30]

What is Proactivity?

Proactivity is the essential state of mind for building your Christlike character. It is the God-given gift to you, allowing you to be in charge of your actions and take responsibility for your life. Proactivity is the mentality and attitude of the new you, as the Holy Spirit is transforming you from a regular Christian into a mighty warrior in Christ. Proactivity refers to anticipatory, change-oriented, and self-initiated behavior in your life.

Proactivity is the inside-out approach initiated by the Holy Spirit in transforming you. Proactivity is the ability to choose your way of thinking, speaking, and acting based on a set of principles that reflect your Christian values. Proactivity always implies a sense of urgency: start the transformation now instead of later. There is no need to wait for future events or some better circumstances; do it now! Proactivity is based on the "I CAN DO IT NOW" credo: I can be more resourceful now, I can be more creative now, and I can be more cooperative now. Proactivity does not suggest being pushy, aggressive, or insensitive. On the contrary, proactivity implies being sensitive and considerate to others. But at the same time, proactive people know how to read reality, figure out what's needed, and act by their values and interests.

One of the best examples of proactivity is the story of Joseph found in the Old Testament. Joseph was sold into slavery in Egypt by his brothers at a young age. Despite his adverse circumstances, Joseph did not languish in self-pity as a slave-servant in the household of Potiphar, nor did he plan revenge on his brothers. Instead, strengthened by his faith in the Lord, Joseph took the higher road. He used a proactive approach to take charge of his life under very adverse circumstances. In a few years of diligent work and impeccable behavior, he was put in charge of his master's household. Then the day came when Joseph was faced again with a difficult moral choice, but he refused to compromise his integrity. As a result, he was unjustly imprisoned for more years. What did he do in prison? Did he fall in despair and depression? Did he start plotting on taking revenge on Potiphar and his wife? Not at all. Again, Joseph used his strong character, diligence, and wits to work his way up again, and soon he was running the prison. And under God's guidance, not long after that, Joseph was running the entire kingdom of Egypt, second only to the Pharaoh. Now, that is a proactive attitude at its best!

"And the LORD was with Joseph, and he was a prosperous man; and he was in the house of his master the Egyptian." (Genesis 39:2)

Why should our goal as Christians be to become proactive? Because the proactive model will:
- Help us become like Jesus
- Help us find faster the purpose of God for us
- Help us cooperate better with the Holy Spirit
- Become the foundation on which the Diamond Soul character is being built.
- Liberate us from any troubled past
- Provide the maximum personal effectiveness in dealing with self and with others

> REMEMBER: PROACTIVITY IS THE
> STATE OF MIND THAT YOU ARE IN CHARGE AND
> RESPONSIBLE FOR YOUR LIFE UNDER THE
> GUIDANCE OF THE HOLY SPIRIT

How to Become Proactive

"Create in me a clean heart, O God; and renew a right spirit
within me. Restore unto me the joy of thy salvation; and
uphold me *with thy* free spirit." (Psalm 51:10-12)

How to transform reactive behavior patterns into proactivity? First
of all, you have to ask for help from the Holy Spirit dwelling inside you.
Second, you have to want it badly and convince yourself about the advantages and liberation it will bring to your life. Repressing an existing reactive
habit and replacing it with a proactive one is not easy. Actually, it is very
hard. It requires close cooperation between you and the Holy Spirit. It
requires a change in paradigm deep inside your mind and soul. But it can
be done if you use self-awareness, imagination, and willpower--the three
divine attributes we humans received from our Creator. The transformation
process requires commitment, diligence, and perseverance. It requires time
and patience. Also, remember that habits are acts done repeatedly, which
means that the new value-driven proactive patterns you want to adopt must
be repeated over and over until they become deeply ingrained in your being.
In this way, they become habits of effectiveness.

Becoming proactive requires significant paradigm shifts about many
things such as time, choices, attitudes, values, and so on. See the table below
for illustration.

SHIFT FROM	SHIFT TO
There is no time.	I will make time.
There is nothing to do.	I have so many things to learn.
It can wait.	I must act now.
Easy	Useful
Procrastination	Urgency
Trivial	Important
Sloppiness	Excellence
Laziness	Dynamic
Unsure	Assertive
I depend on others.	I am self-reliant.
I am moody.	I can control my weaknesses.

To become effective, proactivity must become a new habit embedded deeply in your soul and mind. It must replace the old patterns which are no longer useful and must be discarded. If we look at our brain as a computer, we can say that proactivity is a new version of the mentality software program designed to replace the older outdated version.

Let us explore now what needs to change regarding how a young married couple talks to each other to improve their relationship. Despite their love for each other, the current way of talking is marred by selfishness, blaming each other, impatience, and raised voices. Conversations about mundane issues get quickly out of control, escalating into shouting matches on the sorry state of their marriage. In a sense, the couple magnifies each other's weaknesses, leading to a negative emotional bondage between the two. This bondage must be broken if they want to change the nature of their talks.

Let's assume that the wife is the one who gets trained in proactivity and wants to apply it in conversations with her husband. She needs to be aware of and do the following three things in the sequence indicated below:

1. First, she must stay calm and composed when facing her hubby, regardless of how excited or angry he becomes. In other words, she must be in full control of her emotions. While being in control of hers, the wife should also try to detect and understand the husband's emotional state.

2. Secondly, she must repress her impulses to answer quickly and defensively to her husband's hurting words. She must take several seconds to think before opening her mouth.

3. Thirdly, her considerate response must always be positive, based on love and respect for him. Her words must reflect how much she treasures the marriage, and her body language must display her love for him.

The results of her new way of talking may not show up during the first try, but without question, the husband will notice it. Actually, he may even be suspicious of her motives. But her calmness will surely calm him down, and her loving words for sure will comfort him. So slowly, their conversations will become calmer, more respectful, and meaningful. As a result, the trust in each other will increase, making both of them feel better and better about the marriage. But more on how to conduct proactive conversations with other people will be found later on in this book.

> REMEMBER: NEW PROACTIVE HABITS
> MUST BE REPEATED OVER AND OVER UNTIL
> THEY BECOME FULLY INTERNALIZED.

Is Proactivity Worth the Trouble?

Of course, it is. Adopting a Holy Spirit-inspired proactive mentality means that you can start talking to God about His purpose for your life right away. Every evening you should initiate the sacred conversation with him. Do not wait for future signs; do not expect his special call on you. You take the initiative in talking to him. As one who has been through this process, I can assure you of one thing: you should not doubt that proactivity is part of God's plans for you. Otherwise, you wouldn't think about it, would you?

Becoming proactive will unquestionably have a profound transformative effect on you. From a mostly passive and reactive person right now, you will be slowly turning into a more action-centered and forward-thinking individual. Think about it: in the past, you were looking at life as *"what will it do to me?"* Now, your inner voice is saying, *"what will I make of it?."* Mostly a helpless person at the mercy of worldly circumstances in the past, now you regard yourself as a secure individual in charge of your life. And all will take place under the divine guidance of the Holy Spirit. Isn't it wonderful? You cannot go wrong, can you? Besides, adopting proactivity will open the door to the building and polishing you Diamond Soul character.

> **Nobody can hurt you**
> **without your consent.**
> **Eleanor Roosevelt**

I can also promise that when you become sufficiently proactive, you will:

- Be sure you're following God's plans for your life
- Become a more productive, and humble servant of God
- Let no one and nothing from the temporal world run your life

- Allow no evil person or adverse circumstances to take away your fighting spirit.
- Not lose your Christ-given dignity and faith in God even if you lose all your worldly possessions

---

REMEMBER: BECOMING PROACTIVE MEANS THAT
YOU NOW FOLLOW GOD'S PLAN FOR YOUR LIFE

Since you have embarked on the road of proactivity, would you like to know which another key benefit it will bring to your persona? Hint: it's something immaterial which encircles you and goes with you wherever you travel. It will be unseen, yet people will feel it quickly. Do you know what it is? Read on, and marvel at what you'll find out!

Moments of Reflection

1. Think of several examples of instinctive reactions in the biological world and human behavior. What are their benefits? What are the drawbacks?

2. Examine your behavior for several days and determine if you are mostly a reactive person or a proactive one. How much in you is reactivity, and how much proactivity?

3. Examine yourself and pick up several reactive responses you provide often. Why do you do that? Are they beneficial to you?

4. Construct proactive responses based on your values to replace old reactive responses? What value system will you employ? Why?

5. Do you consider proactivity to be a Fruit of the Spirit? Why?

CHAPTER 6
CIRCLE OF INFLUENCE

———•◆•●•◆•———

"Iron sharpeneth iron; so a man sharpeneth
the countenance of his friend."
(Proverbs 27:17)

Here are some of my favorite quotes on influencing people:

Dale Carnegie: *"The only way to influence people is to talk in terms of what the other person wants."*

Beatrix Potter: *"I hold that a strongly marked personality can influence descendants for generations."*

John Maxwell: *"Leadership is not about titles, positions, or flowcharts. It is about one life influencing another."*

Henry Adams: *"A teacher affects eternity; he can never tell where his influence stops."*

In the previous chapter, we learned about what it means to be proactive. In this one, we will explore together one of the most excellent benefits of proactivity: the ability to influence yourself, other people, and your surroundings.

What is Influence?

Webster's dictionary explains influence as *"the power or capacity of causing an effect in indirect or intangible ways"* and *"an emanation of spiritual or moral power."*[31] In this book, we define it as the ability of proactive people to change things within themselves, within other people, and in their surroundings. The capacity to influence people, events, ways of thinking, and the natural environment is the hallmark of leaders and great people. We should all aspire to acquire this ability.

A useful paradigm to look at your influence upon surroundings is to consider two concentric circles around you.[32] The smaller is called the Circle of Influence. It defines what is within your reach, what you can act upon. The Circle of Influence includes yourself, objects you can touch, people you know, things you do. Proactive people focus their efforts on the Circle of Influence, where they have direct control. In other words, they concentrate their positive energy first on themselves and on what they do, then on the people around them. Thus, when exercising their power of influence, proactive people are enlarging their Circle of Influence.

The larger circle surrounding the first is called the Circle of Concern. It includes a wide range of concerns and interests that we may have regarding critical contemporary issues, such as environmental matters, taxation levels, societal and governance issues, etc. Reactive people are attracted to such broader issues and tend to spend their time and energy in the Circle of Concern. They complain to newspapers, criticize big corporations, write letters to the elected officials, grumble about other people. Their actions may indeed be an expression of frustration in their lives, but unfortunately, their complaints seldom lead to noticeable improvements. In other words, they waste their time. Even worse, lack of results reinforces reactive people's belief that they are victims of a powerful societal conspiracy against them. The blaming and accusing attitudes generate a negative energy around them, which further shrinks their Circle of Influence with other people.

Solving Problems

Let's now look closer at how we, proactive people, should deal with problems. First, we should note that they are of three kinds: (i) problems under our direct control, (ii) problems under our indirect control, or (iii) problems out of our control.

(i) <u>Direct control problems</u> should be solved first because they are within our reach. They may include working on ourselves, such as character building, seeking advice from God, long-term planning, personal management, working on our relationships with loved ones, bettering efficiency at work, and so on. Remember: the first person you influence should be you, the only one who is at the center of your Center of Influence. Initiating the process of personal change and self-growth in Christ will get you onto a positive, ascending spiral of enhanced self-confidence. Work, therefore, daily to change your way of thinking, strengthen your character, and improve your behavior. By only doing these activities, people around you will notice and admire them, and some will instinctively want to emulate you. People are always attracted to good people, so now you are like a magnet to others. By improving yourself, you have already started influencing others. Remember also that wherever you go, you take your Circle of Influence with you. Wherever you happen to be, when you exhibit positive behavior traits such as courtesy, sincerity, humor, optimism, and integrity, as well as all fruits of the Spirit, you will draw people and create a feeling of trust and goodwill toward you. This is the first step toward influencing others!

(ii) <u>Indirect control problems</u> are more challenging to solve because they require specialized skills and higher experience. They're solved most effectively by using new methods of influence. For instance, you want to influence how a particular organization is being run, but realize that traditional methods of persuasion, such as logical arguments, pressure, or even threats do not work. What do you do? Well, using other skills still to be described later on in this material, you should try to formulate new ways of influencing people using win-win strategies, effective communications, and creative, collaborative solutions.

(iii) <u>No-control problems</u> or situations present us with an unusual challenge, because by definition, there is no way to solve them. Then, what do we do? The only thing we can do is what all wise people have done over the centuries: accept them or walk away from them! Accept them with serenity and peace of mind, even with a smile on your face. So, let's share the spirit embodied in the well-known Serenity Prayer.

There are so many ways to work on yourself in the Circle of Influence: become a better listener, be a better student, be a better parent, be more disciplined, be a better boss or employee. And be a happier person! Sometimes, the best proactive thing to do is to be satisfied genuinely, put a big smile on your face, and be grateful to the Almighty for all the blessings he has given you. It may sound strange but happiness, like unhappiness, is a choice. Reactive people may decide to be unhappy because of the bad weather outside. Proactive people carry the mental weather inside them so that they can be happy despite the surroundings. Reactive people feel miserable and alone because of the spiritual vacuum inside their souls. Proactive Christians are never alone because the Holy Spirit is always within them. Isn't that wonderful?

REMEMBER: FOR MAXIMUM EFFECTIVENESS,
CONCENTRATE YOUR ENERGY IN
THE CIRCLE OF INFLUENCE!

Keeping Commitments

At the heart of working effectively in the Circle of Influence is the ability to keep commitments to yourself. A commitment is a promise and a pledge of honor. It is a word given to someone--in this case, yourself--that defines you and represents your honor. Pledges must be kept at all costs because they describe best who you are deep inside your soul. They describe your integrity of character.

Webster's dictionary defines integrity as "steadfast adherence to a moral or ethical code."[33] When you combine the words integrity and character, you get the phrase 'integrity of character.' The integrity of character is the number one indicator of proactive people. It means that someone who lives with integrity lives according to the moral values defined by their character. You cannot be proactive if you do not do what you say and do it ethically. The integrity of character should be a feature you learn early in life and then keep working on it forever. At the beginning of growing in Christ, your integrity has a somewhat limited scope and application. But as you advance, your integrity becomes more and more prevalent and persuasive.

As you start working on your proactivity, focus on using promises and goals. Begin by promising yourself something simple, requiring daily repetition. For instance, you may say, "I will jog fifteen minutes each morning," and start doing it regularly, irrespective of the weather outside or your moods. If it's raining, you jog; if you're sad, you jog; if it's cold, you jog; if you're tired, you jog. After a week or two of daily jogging, you will feel better not only physically, but also emotionally. Why is that? Because you see that you are a person of your word, and you act with integrity. Keeping promises to yourself increases your self-esteem, and your confidence goes higher. Besides, you have converted a promise into a healthy habit that will serve you well for the rest of your life. This is the awesome power of proactivity!

As you move to the next level of training, start using goals. Goals are commitments of a more complex nature whose achievement requires proper planning, longer time, and multi-faceted execution. For example, after you've got into the habit of regular jogging, you tell yourself, "now I want to lose ten pounds in three months." To achieve this goal, you have to plan a new diet, rearrange your daily schedule, and even supplement your daily runs with bi-weekly gym sessions. Your expectation—and goal—is that this set of corresponding actions would get you to lose ten pounds in three months. Now you just have to execute them properly. However, keeping your new daily routine will not be easy, and you may have setbacks. But you have to stay on in, to act on it, because it is in your Circle of Influence. The key to success will be perseverance based on the firm commitment to reach your goal. But once you're there at the higher level, you'll discover a new you, prouder and more confident. Achieving your first goal is the living proof that you are and will be capable of keeping commitments.

There are other unexpected but equally important snowballing effects of achieving your first goal. To begin with, you will place a higher value on yourself. Why is that? Because you realize that the new you is much better than the old you. Therefore, it is much more valuable. You place a high value on yourself now because you know that you can deliver. Also, since you value yourself higher, you will consider yourself a more demanding person. As a result, you will increase the demands of yourself, thus strengthening the integrity of your character. This creates an upward spiral of confidence-building and self-empowerment. The higher your confidence, the higher your integrity of character, and the higher will be your value in your own eyes.

> REMEMBER: INTEGRITY OF CHARACTER IS THE
> VALUE YOU PLACE ON YOURSELF

Initiative

Proactive people are doers; they want to act upon themselves or on their environment. They take personal initiatives and assume full responsibility for their outcomes. They do not wait to be told what to do. Reactive people, in contrast, usually expect to be told what to do. They lack the confidence and courage to initiate something, even if it concerns themselves. Initiatives taken by reactive people tend to be weak, limited in scope, and seldom successful. And of course, if something doesn't work or goes wrong, they blame others.

The ability to judge what needs to be done is called initiative. Proactive people have the mindset of taking charge before others do and using initiative as their primary instrument. Taking the initiative means to be dynamic, same as God is described in the Scriptures. Taking the initiative doesn't mean to be pushy, inconsiderate, or aggressive. It simply means recognizing the responsibility to make things happen and taking the necessary actions.

Taking the initiative is the only effective method of increasing the Circle of Influence with yourself and with others. Taking action is the hallmark of dynamic people. Do you want to change your future? Use initiative! Do you want to influence your coworkers? Use initiative! Do you wish to influence your spouse? Use initiative! Even if your efforts are questionable, there is no need to justify yourself to anyone. If you think it's the right thing to do, do it. Some people will like it, while others may not agree with it. But you must press on because you know it has a higher purpose.

If you want to improve your life, take these initiatives:

- Start a diet/fitness program to improve your health.
- Take new college classes to improve your intellect.
- Start making new friends to improve your socio-emotional life.
- Start attending church regularly to improve your spirituality.

While most of your family, friends, and coworkers may approve of your initiative, some may not understand it; even others may resent you. Don't bother about their lack of encouragement or even sarcastic comments; you just press on. In the end, when everyone sees that you have had the courage and perseverance to go through it, guess who is the hero of the day? It will be you. People will not only admire you; they will want to imitate you. This is how your positive influence works on others!

Risk

However, experience shows that not all initiatives work as expected. We can say the outcome of an action can be of three kinds: (i) positive or as expected, which means success; (ii) somehow as expected, which means an ambiguous or neutral outcome; (iii) negative, which means failure. That's why, before undertaking any initiative, you must first analyze its potential downside or risk. Risk is the probability that an enterprise may have a negative outcome. Risk is part of life; just think of accidents, sickness, and gambling. There are also plenty of hazards in any considerate endeavor taken in areas such as finance, marketing, military, etc. Expressed in mathematical terms, risk can take any value from zero to one, where zero is an absolute failure, and one is an unqualified success. This truth is known in popular culture through expressions like "fifty-fifty chance of success." In our Christian religion, the saying "having faith means taking risks" epitomizes the integral nature of faith and risk.

The perception of risk is highly personal. First, it is a matter of discernment, which is a gift of the Spirit. And secondly, it is an interpretation of reality through your psychological filters. The stock market is an excellent example of how people assess the risk of trading shares in a specific company. Those who buy, think the risk of owning shares is low; those who hold, feel the risk is manageable; while people who sell, assess the risk of holding shares is too high. At an emotional level, taking risks can be challenging and stimulating, but it can also become addictive, as is the case with compulsive gambling. Most regular folks are risk-averse, which means they cannot tolerate any kind of risk.

In contrast, proactive people take calculated risks almost daily as part of their professional or personal life. However, they do this only after performing a risk assessment of the contemplated action. The courage of taking the initiative, therefore, must be balanced by prudence. As you see, here come to interplay two of the seven Christian virtues we've learned about: Courage and Prudence.

> REMEMBER: A PROACTIVE CHRISTIAN MUST
> BE COURAGEOUS AND PRUDENT
> AT THE SAME TIME

Courage and Fear

When dealing with initiatives, proactive people must fight another battle, besides doing a rational benefit and risk analysis. This time it is an emotional battle taking place deep in their souls. It has to do with overcoming fear and finding courage. Courage is essential in everything you contemplate doing. You cannot take even the smallest initiative if you're fearful, and for sure, you need great courage to consider larger ones.

Fear is a deep, visceral feeling in our nervous system. Some call it one of the most primitive and powerful emotions. It alerts us to the presence of danger, and it was critical in keeping our ancestors alive. From the early days of humankind, fear was the trigger mechanism for self-defense, manifested either as preparing for combat or for fleeing. The human body's response to fear can be divided into two stages, biochemical and emotional. The biochemical response is fast and universal, consisting mostly of an adrenaline rush, increased heartbeats, and sweating. In contrast, the emotional response is delayed and is highly individualized. Some people like risky or scary situations and enjoy them as thrill rides. These are "thrill junkies." However, most people are fear-adverse and try to avoid these situations if possible.

Luckily, in our contemporary society, we seldom face survival dangers. However, at a deep instinctual level, most of us still carry some fear. Fear has many manifestations, such as fear of darkness, fear of not succeeding, fear of meeting new people, fear of speaking in public, fear of the unknown, etc. Extreme fears are called traumas or phobias, and may relate to an irrational fear of spiders, snakes, bugs, etc. For most of us, fear or anxiety will negatively affect our personal development and behavior. Being a profoundly intimate emotion, fear is a subject about which people seldom talk. Regardless, if it's real or imaginary, just an anxiety or a debilitating trauma, fear is another hurdle that most of us must overcome as we grow up emotionally.

> **All great deeds are done
> in face of great fear.**
> **Winston Churchill**

Fear can only be conquered by courage. The dictionary defines courage in two crucial ways. First, "the ability to do something that frightens others," and second, "the quality of someone who decides to do something difficult or dangerous, even though they may be afraid."[34] Courage doesn't come from outside; it can originate only from inside us. It comes naturally to some people, but most of us must master it. Courage stems from confidence in your physical, emotional, and intellectual abilities--the conviction that you are a good and worthy person. But above all, it comes from your Christian faith. As such, a Christ-like multifaceted character produces courage because you intrinsically perceive yourself under divine protection, being a righteous individual, and having noble purposes in life.

As it is well known, acts of courage can be seen by others as being heroic or foolish. Heroic acts of courage generally take place in unusual situations such as fire, natural disaster, or time of war. People who do acts of bravery are common people who behave uncommonly when facing danger. Society rewards them with citations and medals, and the popular culture elevates them on the pedestal of heroes to inspire future generations. But showing courage also happens during ordinary life, such as standing up to threatening speech, parents speaking up at a school meeting, or citizens criticizing local authorities. Courage can and should be cultivated and enhanced. For instance, preparation, practice, and meditation is an effective way to overcome the fear of speaking to large groups.

Experience shows that courage relates to "the fighting spirit" in man, which is an emotional state of heightened alertness and combativeness. This is also known as "power state" or "being in the zone." Soldiers, athletes, politicians, performing artists, and salespeople know how to excite themselves up to reach their full competitive potential. Hyped-up techniques may involve special body moves, songs, chants, slogans, team-rituals, etc. The well-known motivational speaker and author Tony Robbins asserts that each of us must discover the techniques to put us in a "power state" before any critical activity.

The Holy Scriptures provide numerous examples of courageous men and women, such as David, John the Baptist, Esther, Deborah, Abigail, and Daniel. They upheld their belief in God despite threats and great adversities.

In this chapter, I hope you have learned to ask new questions about yourself: how do you use your power of influence? Are you a person of initiative? Are you a fearful individual or a man of courage? Do you know how to do a risk-reward analysis? Regardless of what answers you give to the above questions, now is the time to find out where they truly lead you: to find out who you really are. Turn the page to find out the surprising answers!

Moments of Reflection

1.   Think of what kind of people have influenced you in your life so far? Do you regret or cherish their influence?
2.   Do you carry deep inside your soul fears that nobody knows about? Do you wish you can get rid of them?
3.   When was the last time you took an important initiative? How did it turn out?
4.   What's your attitude toward risk? Do you enjoy the 'adrenaline rush' when doing a risky outdoor activity?
5.   Think of how courage, fear and prudence relate to each other
6.   Have you ever set yourself in a "power state"? What did you do to get there? Did you find it useful?

Chapter 7
You are a Righteous Warrior

———•✦•●•✦•———

"Thou therefore endure hardness, as a good
soldier of Jesus Christ." (2 Timothy 2:3)

The Struggle of Life

For nearly all people, life looks difficult most of the time, but sometimes
it is punishing. Every day just seems to be a fight for survival, struggling to
make ends meet. You have money problems, difficulties with relationships,
health troubles, and a multitude of other issues depleting your energy and
enthusiasm. Is this how things are for you? Why is life so strenuous and
unfair, with obstacles popping out before you like mushrooms after rain?

This way of thinking is anchored in the reality of the biological life
where only the fittest survive, as well as in the contemporary human society where daily life is indeed difficult. Phrases like "struggle for existence,"
"make ends meet," "fight for your rights," etc., which are engrained in the
popular vocabulary, reflect this opinion. During man's history, human life
has been perceived as an adversarial, confrontational process in which only
a few people win, and most lose. The majority of people may even think
of life as a constant burden imposed on them by a large, oppressive, and

punishing system. They regard themselves as slaves, and to some extent, they are right. Not a pretty picture!

Fortunately for us, Pastor Rick Warren and psychologist Viktor Frankl each provided new paradigms about the worldly life that are very, very useful. Pastor Warren instructs us to look at life as God wants us to: as a Test, as a Trust, and as a Temporary Assignment.[35]

Life as a <u>Test</u> is a metaphor encountered many times in the Bible. God continually tests people's character, faith, obedience, love, and loyalty. Just think of Abraham, Joseph, Ruth, and Daniel. Why does God do that? Because through these stories, God tells us that all of life is a test, and character is both developed and revealed by tests. We cannot possibly know all the tests God will send our way, but the Scriptures give us substantial clues. For sure, they will include delayed promises, impossible problems, unanswered prayers, undeserved criticism, and even senseless tragedies. The takeaway? Nothing is insignificant in our lives. Even the smallest incident has a purpose for our development as children of God. Some tests seem overwhelming, while others you won't even notice. But all of them have eternal implications.

Life as a <u>Trust</u> tells us that our time on earth, our energy, intelligence, resources, wealth, relationships, and opportunities are all gifts from God, simply entrusted to us through his grace. We are merely stewards of whatever God gives us. We own nothing; we create nothing. But God expects us to be good caretakers of his property, and to grow ourselves in doing so. For this reason, at the end of our life on earth, we will be evaluated according to how well we handled God's trust.

Life as a <u>Temporary Assignment</u> is based on the Biblical truth that the permanent, eternal home of believers is in heaven, not on the earth. Earth is just a temporary residence given to us by God to fulfill His plans for humanity. And God warns us not to become too attached to the temporal world, because it is not our real home. One could argue even that God allows us to feel discontent and dissatisfied in the temporal life on purpose.

In the secular sphere, Victor Frankl pioneers a new niche in psychotherapy called logotherapy, to teach us something more practical about how to regard life's struggle. In a nutshell, he states that logotherapy "focuses on the meaning of human existence as well as on man's search for such a meaning"[36] These new words define why we must struggle, thus giving reasons and hope unique to each individual to carry on despite difficulties. For instance, you can say now that "I struggle for my religious freedom," or "I fight for my family," or "I keep going because this is my duty."

However, answers to the why question do not come easily. To find the "meaning, duty, and purpose" of life, to find hope, you must ask your Creator. It is part of your transformational process from a lost soul into a believer. In cooperation with the Holy Spirit, you must search your soul, struggle with yourself, and conquer yourself. Not only once, but perhaps several times during your life. But when you see the light, when you find the answers, they will give you purpose and direction in life. And you know that they are in line with God's plans for you. They will keep you going when you are tired, or things turn against you. By providing the reasons and hope for the struggle, you take the battle itself to a higher level. Struggle is no more an act of physical and biological survival; it becomes a burning fire at a spiritual, intellectual, and emotional level. It becomes your reason for being; it defines who you are and what you stand for! We will learn more about these concepts as we come to study Stepping Stone 3.

Diamond Soul proposes that a better paradigm for looking at the temporal life should read like this: "I am a Christian blessed by the Lord with the gift of life, the trust of life and the test of life on this earth. For this reason, I fully enjoy the life given to me by the Almighty and do my best to detect and fulfill the plans he has ordained for me. I look at life with serenity and confidence because I know that all difficulties are nothing, but tests and trials meant by the Lord to teach, strengthen, and humble me."

REMEMBER: LIVE YOUR TEMPORARY
LIFE WITH PASSION, DIGNITY AND
HUMILITY FOR THE GLORY OF GOD

The Inner Struggle

"The LORD *is* my shepherd; I shall not want...I will fear no evil: for thou *art* with me" (Psalm 23:1-4)

The inner struggle is really what the life of a Christian is all about. It's about facing our hidden adversaries, flexing our spiritual muscles, and giving it all we have, our very best shot. The reality is we all have internal angels and demons to contend with until our final breath. We all have weaknesses and strengths to restrain, balance, or enforce. The struggle inside us is the toughest and longest of all battles we are called to do. Why is that? Because we have to deal with our weaknesses, our insecurities, and our vices.

Deep inside our souls, we have to wage and win the most difficult battle. We have to choose between right and wrong, good and evil, virtues and vices. These will be impossible choices for the Fallen Man, unless he has a guiding light. Fortunately for us, we believers have the divine guidance provided by our faith in Jesus Christ. Through teaching, we learn what to choose to please God. Through faith, we learn why this is the right choice. But how do we go about doing it practically and effectively? Here is where the teachings from Diamond Soul come in. They provide authoritative answers to the how question in the form of clear, logical, and common -sense step-by-step instructions you just need to follow.

Diamond Soul is a field manual on waging spiritual battles in the trenches. Diamond Soul is a competent companion, supplement, and accessory to your Christian faith. Its competence stems from using the latest findings of modern science, particularly neuropsychology, to understand what's going on in your brain when you undergo a transformation. Thus, you are assured that what you're learning in this material has not only a Biblical foundation, but also a solid scientific base.

Billy Graham, the "pastor of America," reminds us that we have two natures within us, both struggling for mastery: one is spiritual; the other is sinful.[37] Which one will dominate? It depends on which one we feed most. If we feed our spiritual nature and allow the Holy Spirit to empower us, the spirit will rule. If we starve our spiritual nature and instead feed the sinful nature, the flesh will dominate. In the New Testament, the apostle Paul talks of every Christian being in an intense spiritual battle. "For we wrestle not against flesh and blood, but against principalities, against powers, against the rulers of the darkness of this world, against spiritual wickedness in high *places*." (Ephesians 6:12)

REMEMBER: CONDUCT YOUR INNER STRUGGLE
UNDER THE GUIDANCE OF THE HOLY SPIRIT

The Outer Struggle

The outer struggle is with the world around us. It is our dealings with the family, friends, co-workers, fellow churchgoers, neighbors, authorities, and so on. It is our efforts to understand the world around us, what it means to us, how it works, and how we can contribute to society. In other words, it is how we see ourselves as Christians in the temporal world and how we relate to it. We know that the role of Christians in the world is twofold: to minister our fellow believers, and to carry out the mission to spread the Good News to unbelievers. Since dealing with our fellow believers should not be considered a struggle, let's focus now on our mission.

Let your light so shine before men,
that they may see your good works,
and glorify your Father which is in heaven.
Matthew 5:16

The world is the social battlefront where we believers must battle sin, and evil confronting us from the outside. It is a battleground where external powers, values, influences, and temptations are in conflict with our faith and assault us from all directions. As we do battle, the Bible admonishes us to be in the world but not to become of the world. And to resist the pressure of an unredeemed society that would force us into its mold. Apostle Paul wrote of this great conflict in 2 Corinthians 10:4–5, where he describes worldly convictions, habits, thoughts, and affections held by society, by culture, and by humanity as a whole. These are worldly because they oppose God, deny God, or attempt to exist apart from God.

For you, as a Christian warrior, the outer struggle is the arena in which you display who you are and act under the teachings of your faith. Your primary role as an influencer of people is an example of your character and behavior. At the same time, you express with courage your views on matters of culture that you know are detrimental or harmful to young people. Your outer struggle signifies your commitment to actively participating in the life of the organization you belong to, be it the workplace, school, or church. It indicates your willingness to help others who are weak or disadvantaged or have fallen on hard times.

> REMEMBER: YOUR CHARACTER AND BEHAVIOR ARE YOUR BEST WEAPONS IN BATTLING THE WICKEDNESS OF THE TEMPORARY WORLD

Standing on Stepping Stone 2

"And the angel of the LORD appeared unto him, and said unto him, The LORD *is* with thee, thou mighty man of valour." (Judges 6:12)

Now, as you have reached the second stepping stone on your journey, you should rest a bit and reflect on what you have learned so far: who you are, your new proactive mentality, and your circle of influence. Being proactive is the most fundamental attribute of your new mindset. It is the expression of the divine nature of man, of his unlimited capacity for self-knowledge and self-reliance. Being proactive gives birth to the warrior spirit in you, which will see you through all adversities in life, and the process will strengthen you. The bigger the misfortune, the heavier the burden; the more intense pressure upon you, the stronger your character will become. As a diamond is created in nature by the immense pressures and temperatures deep inside the earth, so deep in your soul, a raw diamond is being born during the struggle for self-discovery and growth. This natural diamond will turn itself in time into a shining, multifaceted

Diamond Soul, the ultimate expression of your character, as we will see in upcoming chapters.

Can the attribute of proactivity be acquired in a more relaxed, faster way, or even be inherited? Not at all; this is not possible. Proactivity can only be bought with sweat, tears, and blood. Each person must earn it through a painful and prolonged inner struggle. If you want to become a true man of character, an independent man, you must learn and internalize proactivity through a deliberate, methodical, and systematic endeavor under your total control. And only under the guidance and with the full cooperation of the Holy Spirit.

From this point on, you must see yourself in a new light: you are now a mighty Christian Warrior, a fighter for a noble cause. You get inspiration from Jesus Christ himself, whose character attributes of strength, firmness, courage, and patience will surely enter your nature under his divine guidance. This new paradigm about self will take you closer to God, will put you on a higher moral plateau, and it will make you stand out of the crowd. At the same time, it will increase your humility before God and fellow men.

Now, as you stand on Stepping Stone 2, you can graciously thank God for the knowledge he has let you acquired so far. And you can tell yourself:

- I know that I am a humble soldier of Christ.
- I know that I am under divine command and protection.
- I draw my inner power from my faith. I use the Holy Spirit in me to fight the sinful nature of man that is also in me.
- I cherish and value my Christian virtues of Prudence, Responsibility, Fortitude, and Courage.
- I do battle with the world's dark forces, to defend and advance the Christian principles of life.
- I know my strengths and shortcomings.

- I am determined to better myself every day and to continue working on my Diamond Soul character.
- I know how to fight: I am proactive, I take the initiative, and I am committed.
- I have courage: I am brave, I am confident, and I am proud of myself.
- I am principled: I conduct myself based on time-tested Biblical principles.
- I am humble in victory and undeterred in defeat.
- I have fun: life is a blessing, and the Lord is my joy!

Stepping Stone 2 is the first step in becoming proactive and knowing who you are. It must be followed by learning how to search for and define the meaning of your life. Of course, based on your conversations with the Almighty. This is described in the upcoming Stepping Stone 3 titled "This Is Your Godly Way." Then, equally important, come the teachings of Stepping Stone 4 "You are Disciplined," which will enhance your self-discipline and train your willpower. Once you learn and internalize the principles advocated in these great stepping stones, you will be almost done with crafting and polishing the many facets of your Diamond Soul character.

CONGRATULATIONS: YOU ARE NOW A RIGHTEOUS WARRIOR IN CHRIST!

Are you ready to move on? Then turn the page and start climbing toward Stepping Stone 3 called "This is Your Godly Way." Be prepared to learn new things - some of which you've never heard of!

Moments of Reflection

1. Has your life been hard or easy so far? Why?

2. Do you accept the premise that life is a temporary assignment, a trust, and a test?

3. Have you ever asked yourself if your life needs direction, purpose, and meaning?

4. Meditate about the concept of the inner struggle. Does it make sense to you?

5. Have you been aware so far about your outer struggle?

6. What's the main achievement of having reached Stepping Stone 2?

YOUR GODLY WAY

—◆•◆•◆—

Virtues: Hope, Perseverance, Justice

"For I know the plans I have for you, declares the Lord, plans for welfare and not for evil, to give you a future and a hope." (Jeremiah 29:11)

CHAPTER 8
LOOK BACK TO SEE AHEAD

"The steps of a [good] man are ordered by the LORD:
and he delighteth in his way" (Psalms 37:23)

S tepping Stone 3 is the platform on which we learn about planning our lives in accordance with God's intentions for us. Stepping Stone 3 represents the Christian virtues of hope, perseverance, and justice. It is also called the platform of personal leadership because it teaches us how to set the direction and choose proper moral values for the journey of life. These are the most fundamental issues of life that should matter to us. Secular culture tells us we should "keep up with the Joneses," struggle to get higher and higher in status and reputation, and show off our wealth. But we know these are empty and meaningless goals. It is not how well we live, how famous or rich we are, and what people say about us that counts before God. What counts before him is only if we walk in the path of righteousness. Stepping Stone 3 is giving us practical advice and encouragement on how to do that.

In this chapter, we will review the concept of the timeline of life, the principle of double creation and the notion of the path in life. But before we do that, let's listen first what Luke says about walking on God's way, and then read to the parable of the Lost Son.

*"Dear Lord, ...Take that burden from me and replace it with the comfort of your love. Help me to return to you. Hold my hand as **I walk on your path of life**. I choose today to trust in your unfailing love. In Jesus' name, Amen."* (Luke 15)

Parable of the Lost Son:

This is the story of a father whose son chooses to leave the righteous path the father has planned for him. The father has hopeful dreams, but his son has other ideas and wants to run his own life. So, this wise father lets his son go his own way. It's not what the father wants, and it grieves him to allow this, but the father also knows that he can't force his son to choose his plans. He knows his son will have to make his own decision about accepting his father's dreams for him.

Many years have passed. Then one night, the father's heart leaps; for a long way off he sees a figure approaching. His son has returned! He can't run fast enough to meet and to embrace his son. This is the tale of our heavenly Father and how he loves each of us. There's nowhere we can go that his loving arms cannot reach us and rescue us with his love. Wherever we've wandered, even if only in our thoughts and hearts, the Father longs for us to return. He has good plans for our lives that can be trusted.[38]

The Timeline of Life

Let's draw a horizontal line and define its origin to the left as the time of your birth; then, select an arbitrary point on it as the now moment; and finally, extend the line to the right, and call its end the time of your death. You have created the timeline of your life on this earth. This timeline shows how you move from one season to another over time. Related to the passage of time, there are three terms of importance: past, present, and future, which we should explore. These terms have concerned philosophers for millennia. Aristotle (384 BC–322 BC), the great Greek thinker of antiquity, calls this sequence the basic definition of time. He notes that the past has been but is no more, and that future will be but is not yet. In a fascinating way, Aristotle asserts that present actually does not exist because it is a mere invisible and indivisible instant on the endless time axis of past and future. Despite of this, Aristotle states that actually humans live only in the present and, therefore, it alone should be of interest to them.[39]

Let's now examine the past-present-future concept of time from a more pragmatic perspective. This should give us a better understanding of the progression of life on the continuum of time.

The past is the time gone by, it's the life lived so far, and it's what's left behind us. Most of the past lives vividly in our heads as images that are reasonably clear and well-defined. They constitute the universe of thoughts and feelings permanently engraved in our being, thus making us what we currently are. Some memories make us feel good, others make us regret what we did, and others still pain us badly. We can say that memories are the intellectual and emotional baggage we carry with us since early childhood. Regardless, if it's a burden or inspiration, the luggage of the past cannot be left behind; it will always be with us.

The present is the current moment in time; it is today, it is this year. It is where our life is unfolding right now, with all its ups and downs. The present sometimes seems clear and favorable, but other times may look uncertain and threatening. Why is that? Because as we look at the events taking place now, we interpret them through the psychological filters unique to each of us. These filters make up our mentality, which has been created by our own past experiences. Therefore, our mindset becomes the primary factor in our interpretation of the events of the present. This explains why people around us may have a completely different read than ours on the quality of times in which we're living. While we may like the present time, others may hate it. The past may be a drag on our present, or it may be a blessing. Some believe the main reason why so many people fail to move forward in life is because their past creates a mental barrier to future success. However, others see the past as the principal source of their current accomplishments. It is clear, therefore, that although we cannot change the past, we can change our interpretation of it. And this will make all the difference.

The future is the time still to come; it is the day after today, it is next month, it is next year. The future is unknowable to man; only the eternal Almighty who created it can know it. We can only try to forecast it based on our past experiences and imagination. The future becomes, therefore, only a mental image in our head. For this reason, it looks distant, uncertain, and foggy. In fact, by projecting past and present thoughts into the future, we expect them to continue being valid. If our current beliefs are negative, the future will look harmful and undesirable. In contrast, if our current mentality is positive, the future will look positive and attractive. The question then becomes, *"how can a person with a negative mentality create a positive image of the future?"* And the answer is, *"only by changing his/her mentality."* Change of paradigm is the necessary transformational event that will let people project a positive future, a positive path in life. And in doing so, they create a blueprint for building the future according to their dreams.

Stepping Stone 3 encourages us to look at past, present, and future holistically, as a continuum on which our life evolves harmoniously. The past is the foundation on which we build the present, and the present is the base on which we imagine the future. We can say, therefore, that our path in life is the continuous link between these three seasons of time, the thread that provides their interconnectivity.

Learn from the Past

Quite a few people consider they've had a troubled past because specific memories still hound them to this day. In a sense, they feel chained emotionally to their past. To break these chains, they must learn to examine the past rationally and constructively and draw lessons from it. So, the first step in the process of self-examination is to ask quality questions about your past experiences.

The answers you give to good, quality questions will help to understand your past better, and therefore to understand yourself better. In the field of Mathematics, there is the saying, "a problem well formulated is half-solved." The same is also true is in the process of self-analysis. For instance, will a question like *"how come I was so unlucky?"* make you search for an intelligent answer? No, it won't. In contrast, the question *"what lesson did I learn from my failures?"* would inevitably lead you to an enlightening remedy if you are honest enough with yourself. The great thing about using a rational line of examining your past is that it will unveil how the past can become a relevant guide for your future. Learning from the past and applying these lessons to the future is one of the secret keys to personal growth.

Many people have difficulties dealing with a negative past, particularly if it includes traumatic experiences, shame, guilt, anxiety, or phobias. The luggage of their bad memories is too large and heavy, crippling them in what they want to do presently and in the future. These people must try to mitigate the effect of bad memories. Addressing past traumatic experiences should be done promptly, preferably under professional guidance.

> REMEMBER: MAKE YOUR PAST A FRIEND
> AND TEACHER, NOT A TORMENTOR!

Principle of Double Creation

The principle of double creation means that in the human world, all things are created twice: there is an intellectual creation first, followed by a physical creation. Before we do something, we must think about it. Humans visualize their plans first, then execute them. We all have heard of the saying, "He who fails to plan, plans to fail." So true! For instance, before you build a house, you must first prepare the architectural sketches about how the house will look like. Then, you must draw the blueprints according to which the builder will erect it. The preparation of blueprints is a mental creation, it is an intellectual activity. It requires a thinking process. As you start the second creation, the actual building of the house, the carpenters use blueprints every day to guide them to complete the project.

Stepping Stone 3 describes processes based on the principle of double creation: think first, act second. This principle is manifest in all aspects of our lives: plan a trip first, then do it; plan a meal first, then cook it; prepare a business plan first, then execute it. The same holds for your life: plan it first, then live it! Visualize your path in life first, then start the journey! Understanding the principle of the two creations and accepting the responsibility for both, you act within and enlarge the borders of your circle of influence. As long as you include God's purpose for your life in your plans, success will be secured. However, if you do not operate in harmony with this principle, you expose yourself to risks and failure. Unfortunately, most people do not plan their lives properly, or even worse, do not plan at all. These people just exist; they do not live. Consequently, they go through life with no direction, without purpose, and with no end in sight.

> REMEMBER: PLAN YOUR LIFE IN ACCORDANCE
> WTIH GOD'S PURPOSE FOR IT

The Path in Life

What is a path? Every traveler knows a path is the road on the ground that takes you from a starting point to the endpoint of your journey. Similarly, if you think of life as a journey in time, not in space, then it must have a starting point in time, a path to take you to where you want to go, and an endpoint in time. From a biological viewpoint, the starting point for us human is the birth, the journey is the life, and the end of the trip is the end of life. So, the path in life is the journey in time during one's life.

For us believers, the above definitions are correct except for the starting point. Instead of being one's biological birth, the starting point relates to our spiritual rebirth. This is when we experience the transformational event of accepting Jesus Christ in our life as Lord. After we get born again spiritually, our life takes a new meaning; it gets a new purpose and direction. As we've seen earlier, God has five life purposes for us: to worship him, to love others, to be like Christ, to do ministry, and to spread the Good News. We call these primary or doctrinal purposes as the Christian doctrine prescribes them. However, on how we accomplish these primary purposes, God entrusts us to determine on our own. Remarkably, God also leaves it up to our free will to decide what other things are needed to fulfill the specific purposes of ours as unique individuals. And here it is where Stepping Stone 3 comes to be so useful: it provides accurate and practical ways for finding the secondary purposes in our life. These can take the shape of what career to choose, when and whom to marry, where we want to live, and so on. In full concord with the Christian doctrine, we assert that the path in life should provide answers not only to which direction we take, but also how to get there. The course in life must, therefore, be accompanied by a set of moral values to guide us during our life's journey.

Whereas ye know not
what shall be on the morrow...
James 4:14

Getting a sense of one's path in life is not easy. It requires a desire to understand its meaning; it necessitates lengthy soul-searching and answering many difficult own questions. It can only be done under the guidance of the Holy Spirit. People usually think about their path in life when they come out of their youth years after they have been through some personal turmoil and have gained experience. But as a general rule, the soul-searching should start as early as possible.

One useful visualization exercise in sensing your path in life is to go with your mind's eyes to the end of your life and look back. I call this "Look back to see ahead." Imagine yourself on your death bed many years from now, surrounded by family, and contemplating your life. You know you're getting close to meeting your Creator; you know that Judgement Day is nearing. As you lay there, ask yourself these questions: Was I a good Christian? Did I walk in the path of righteousness? Did I have worthy goals in life? Was mine a purposeful life or a wasted one? If I were to re-live it, how would I change it? Was I a good son, husband, and father? Was I a good co-worker, friend, and benefactor?

If you participate seriously in this visualization experience, you will touch for a moment some of your deep, most sacred values. You will confer with the Holy Spirit, who will tell you what God's expectations for your life are. As soon as you return from this imaginary travel in time, think about what you saw, think about your faults and admissions, and write them down. If you were unhappy with your life as a Christian, resolve to improve it from this point on. If you were too self-absorbed a person, decide to correct it from this point forward. If you neglected your family, commit to introduce better balance in your life. If you were an authoritarian boss, pledge to become a better one. In this way, you give yourself the unique opportunity to introduce corrections in real life still to come. In other words, you will visualize a better path for your future life.

> REMEMBER:THE PATH IN LIFE IS THE
> DIRECTION AND SET OF MORAL VALUES
> GUIDING YOU IN YOUR LIFE'S JOURNEY

Are you ready to turn the page? If yes, go right ahead to see what personal leadership is all about. Even if you thought you were a leader, you would uncover new things about you.

Moments of Reflection

1. In a quiet place, relive your life so far: What makes you proud of? What are your major regrets? What are your most disturbing emotional memories?

2. Where did your path in life take you so far? How do you want to better it to the end of it?

3. Which do you think are God's plans for your life? Why do you think so?

4. Try to visualize your future life to its very end. What should be its moral guidelines?

CHAPTER 9
PERSONAL LEADERSHIP

—•◆•◆•◆•—

"...our inner self is being renewed day
by day." (2 Corinthians 4:16)

I n this chapter, we're going to review the concept of life roles, what personal leadership is all about, what is the difference between leadership and management, and what is the mission and meaning in life.

Here is one of my favorite stories about personal leadership:

"On the 15th January 2009, US airways flight 1544 lost power to both engines shortly after take-off from LaGuardia Airport after striking a large flock of geese. The captain, Chesley Sullenberger, realizing they would not make it back to an airport, landed the plane on the Hudson River and saved the lives of the 155 passengers and crew. He remained calm at all times, despite describing it as 'the worst sickening, pit-of-your-stomach, falling-through-the-floor feeling' he had ever experienced. The captain was the last to leave the plane after ensuring no one was left aboard. Later on, this act of heroic leadership was made into a movie, with Tom Hanks portraying the character of Captain Sullenberger".[40]

Sullenberger's role as the captain of the airliner placed his squarely in a leadership position when the accident happened. He not only made the right decision landing the plane on the water, but then he and the crew carried the emergency evacuation plans with calm and professionalism. He was the last one to leave the sinking plane. Captain Sullenberger is the perfect example of a man showing great personal courage in times of crisis.

On the Stage

Some people think that life is the stage of a live theater where we're all actors playing roles according to the script assigned to us by the playwright. Are they right? Yes and no. Yes, because we indeed play many roles in life, and no, because most parts are not necessarily imposed on us, but rather selected according to our God-given free-will. Why is role-playing so important? Because roles are the only venues where we reveal, practice, and hone our inner character. Our character should not be just a fuzzy ideal in our head, but a clear set of rules on how to behave. Our character should exteriorize and manifest itself through our daily behavior. And, our behavior should be the living and breathing expression of our character.

It is obvious that our roles in life change with the seasons of time. For instance, when we are young, we play the roles of children and grandchildren. Later on, we take the roles of spouses and parents, and finally that of grandparents. Consequently, we must define and manage them differently from one season to another. The process of handling life's roles and establishing goals within each part is a process of personal progress and self-growth. Self-growth is, therefore, a process of perpetual renewal under the guidance of the Holy Spirit and your leadership. Renewal is the ability to create, in a conscious way, a new you during each significant period in your life. It must happen in all four dimensions of life: physical, emotional, intellectual, and spiritual. Your renewal as a person is also very much aligned with how the biological life renovates itself since most cells in the human body die and form again every seven years.[41] So, if you do not restore yourself regularly, you will remain an old self in a new biological body every seven years! Just ask yourself, does it make sense to stay a child in a teenage body? Or a teenager in an adult body? Of course, it does not!

REMEMBER: WE ALL PLAY DIFFERENT ROLES IN LIFE THAT CHANGE WITH THE SEASONS OF TIME

What is Personal Leadership?

Visualize Your Direction in Life

In the previous stepping stone, you learned who you are: a warrior in Christ, a soldier of the Christian faith, a fighter for what you believe in. In other words, you defined yourself. Personal leadership takes the definition of yourself a step further. It enhances it by articulating a clear vision for your path in life and prepares you for converting it into reality. Personal leadership is how you drive yourself, how you motivate yourself, and how you measure yourself on the trajectory of self-growth.

> Personal leadership is the process of keeping your vision and values before you, and aligning your life to be congruent with them.
> Dr. Steven R. Covey

Personal leadership is the ability to visualize your direction in life under God's plans for you and to move in that direction with consistency and clarity. Personal leadership is the vital capacity for focusing attention on what matters most, leading your life in the footsteps of Christ. It is how you see yourself today, tomorrow, next year, and next decade. A useful view about yourself has to be rooted in your past; it must address the future, and deal with today's realities. It represents who you are and what you stand for. The view about yourself must be inspiring and compelling, yet realistic.

The Road Not Taken

Personal leadership is also the ability to manage two opposing forces that continuously act upon us in life. The first force pushes us in an unknown direction, it makes us drift in life, and it compels us to go with the flow. It consists of the ups and downs of life, which are the result of an adverse socio-economic environment, and our internal weaknesses. The first force is the worldly force, which generally opposes everything you wish to do. In contrast, the second force is the force of free will, which is under the control of the Holy Spirit and your personal leadership. It is the force of divine guidance. The second force must overcome the opposing resistance put up by the first force and to move us in the direction determined by God's plan. As poet Robert Frost (1874-1963) put it so well in his famous poem titled "The Road not Taken"[42]

> *"Two roads diverged in the wood,*
> *And sorry I could not travel both*
> *So, I took the one less traveled*
> *And that has made all the difference."*

Personal leadership is the solemn oath a believer takes after receiving the Holy Spirit in his heart, *"to repent and serve my Lord and Savior Jesus Christ."* Personal leadership is when a boy of eleven tells his friends, *"I want to become a teacher like my father,"* or a young woman promises herself, *"my calling is to serve as a missionary in Guatemala,"* or a retired person who commits himself *"to helping the needy."* But personal leadership is also the strength of a teenager who tells his peers, *"I do not want to smoke or do drugs."*

Use your Imagination

How do you visualize your future? How do you ensure it becomes a reality? By using your imagination and discipline. For instance, if you want to become a doctor, you must first view yourself as a student in pre-med college, then attending a medical school, then doing your residency duties, and finally taking the exams prescribed by the board in your state. At the same time, you have to figure out how to finance so many years of study without taking debilitating personal loans.

We Christians must have a clear view as to where we are heading to fulfill the purposes of God for us. Our role calls us to be awake and alive in Jesus through the power of the Holy Spirit. Why is that? Because we want to make a positive difference in a cynical world. Let's remember an essential truth about unbelievers: they do not read the Bible, but they study us Christians all the time! When in contact with them, we have the perfect chance to talk and influence them through our behavior. Considering it, they will see how different we are from most other people they meet. And they will want to know why we are different and what makes us so unique. They will come to talk to us! What a great occasion to open their minds and influence them!

REMEMBER: PERSONAL LEADERSHIP IS THE
ABILITY TO VISUALIZE A CLEAR PATH FOR YOUR
FUTURE TRUE TO GOD'S PURPOSE FOR YOUR LIFE

Leadership or Management?

Stepping Stone 3 defines the principles of personal leadership, while the subsequent platform of knowledge Stepping Stone 4 deals with the laws of personal management. Why are these two platforms organized this way? Because leadership is the first creation and should be studied first, whereas management is the second creation and should be studied second. Before we build something, we first must view it in our minds. Leadership creates a vision; management brings it to reality. Before we manage something, we must first define what that is. This is in contrast to what most people believe, namely, that the words leadership and management mean the same and are interchangeable. They are not. Leadership is not management, and management is not leadership, as we shall see shortly.

In the words of the famous management consultant and author Peter Drucker (1909-2005), *"Leadership is doing the right things; management is doing things right."*[43] Leadership asks the question what; management asks the question how. In business, leadership deals with the top line: What are the things we want to do? Management, however, has a bottom-line focus: How can we accomplish those things most economically?

Life shows that we, individuals, families, or larger groups, are often so busy doing the daily tasks that we don't even realize we are going in circles. In other words, we're busy doing wrong or irrelevant things, focusing on matters that matter least. Let's be honest: How many of us find ourselves toiling day and night, yet the results we are hoping for fail to materialize? How many of us have worked on improving ourselves for many years, but we appear to be stagnant? That is why we require a vision, a destination, or a compass to show us the right direction. Only leadership can do that. Effectiveness with myself does not solely depend on how much effort I expend, but on whether or not I spend it in the right direction. So, as individuals, we must use personal leadership to establish what we want to do. Only after that, we should use our management skills to ensure our efforts will take us toward the desired goals in the most efficient manner. But we'll discuss more about personal management when we reach the next stepping stone titled, *I am Disciplined*. In the meantime, it suffices to look at the table below, which contrasts the approaches taken by leadership and management with regards to category issues.

Category Issue	Management	Leadership
People	Subordinates	Followers
Direction	Existing path	New roads
Method	Formal, rational	Passionate, emotional
Essence	Stability	Change
Culture	Execute & maintain	Shape
Rules	Make	Break
Style	Transactional	Transformational
Decision	Make	Facilitate

We cannot conclude our discussion about personal leadership without addressing two fundamental concepts related to it. The first one is the meaning of life, which addresses the question *"What is human existence?"*, a question as old as humanity itself. And the second one is the mission in life, which addresses the inquiry *"why am I on this earth,"* which also it is as old as human civilization. Let's look at them briefly.

Meaning of Life

Meaning is another critical concept about life. It is a challenging, abstract idea that has preoccupied thinkers from most civilizations over thousands of years. The search for life's meaning has produced much philosophical, theological, scientific, and metaphysical body of thought throughout history. The definition of life, or the answer to the question *"What is human life?"* pertains to the significance of existence in general and the mystery of human living in particular. It is specific to each culture, each epoch, and even to each individual. Why is the question about existence so tricky? It all starts with the fact that life itself has different definitions in the eyes of different people. For many, life is all about family and love. For others, life is about faith and service. For others still, life is about survival in an adversarial world. Or, about acquiring riches and glory. Or about leaving a legacy.

In the Western culture, the search for the meaning of life is best captured in Prince Hamlet's introspective monologue from the play written by William Shakespeare (1564-1616) over four hundred years ago[44]:

> *"To be, or not to be, that is the question:*
> *Whether 'tis nobler in the mind to suffer*
> *The slings and arrows of outrageous fortune,*
> *Or to take arms against a sea of troubles,"*

From a Christian perspective, meaning in life is not found only in accepting Jesus as Savior, as wonderful as that is. Instead, the real purpose in life is when one begins to follow Christ as his disciple, learning of him, spending time with him in his Word, communing with Him in prayer, and walking with him in obedience to his commands.

To inquire insistently about the meaning of life, might mark you out as being somewhat introspective, weird, or even naive. Why is that? Because people nowadays often say–– sometimes in a sad way, other times more cynically––that life just has no meaning. This is not true. The Bible teaches us that life does have substantial meaning and wondering about the meaning of life is an essential spiritual and intellectual activity. To support this way of thinking, all principled teachings in this book outline a range of practical steps that we can take to ensure we lead the lives of maximal meaningfulness.

> REMEMBER: MEANING OF LIFE IS YOUR VERY
> PERSONAL ANSWER TO THE QUESTION
> "WHAT IS HUMAN LIFE?"

Mission in Life

For us Christians, the word mission has a particular spiritual resonance. It evokes our duty to go out in the world to spread the Good News, which we discussed at length in one of the preceding chapters. In this section, therefore, we will look at other important sense of the phrase "mission in life" strictly from a secular perspective. Webster's dictionary has several definitions for mission in life: *"anything you pursue with almost religious fervor,"*; *"an allotted or self-imposed duty of great importance to you,"*; a *"supreme calling."*[45] We can say that the mission in life is the deep calling you have in your DNA, which defines you as a person and infuses all aspects of your life. A mission isn't something an outside force assigns you but rather something you assign yourself. It is a perfect example of proactivity. Because it comes from within us, it serves as the reason we engage in various value-making activities throughout our lives like practicing medicine, writing books, or serving in the military. For example, you may choose a career in education because you've made it your mission to inspire children to reach their potential. Or you might choose a career as a pastor because you want to spread the word of God and to shepherd your flock.

> **To be what we are,**
> **and to become what we**
> **are capable of becoming,**
> **it is the only end in life.**
> **Robert Luis Stevenson**

<u>Your Talents</u>

How do you find and define your mission in life? You must search for it by tapping into your God-given talents and intuition, again, under the guidance of the Holy Spirit. Discover as early as possible what you're good at, then cultivate and sharpen your talents. This means that as a teenager, you must expose yourself to as many fields of study, issues, and situations as possible, and figure out what excites you. Are you a quick wit and good with numbers? Keep developing these talents and look for a career in science, engineering, or business. Do you like arts and are good at it? Then you should consider a career in this field. Are you more an introverted person inclined to contemplation and meditation? Then your calling may be in the spiritual realm, like theology or preaching.

You must search for your inner gifts, you must strive to discover them.[46] Inner gifts are not invented, they are detected. If we search for them, if we find them and know how to use them--then we are halfway on defining our mission in life. Keep in mind that talents fall into two categories: early talents, also called inner gifts, and later talents. Early talents are those very visible since childhood and youth, such as physical abilities, musical skills, agility with numbers, good memory, the capacity to speak, and write well, etc. Later talents show up a bit later on in life, such as relating well to people, having the power of persuasion, displaying empathy for others, having personal charisma, etc.

Here are three practical questions to ask when you start searching for your gifts from God[47]:

(i) What thrilled you as a child?

Take a few minutes to recall your most joyous memories from elementary school. What made those moments so enjoyable? Which were the common threads? As you ponder these childhood memories, consider what similar activities thrill you as an adult. Why are you better at some things than others? Look for the common theme of thrilling activities way back in childhood and now as an adult, and you will find that unique talent palette that defines you. There's only a 1-in-33- million chance you have the same top five talent set as another person! This makes you so unique! Those school memories reveal what your deep abilities are. Today, find ways to slant your work toward those moments that thrilled you yesterday.

(ii) What makes you lose track of time?

Let's say you have half a Saturday all for yourself at home and begin a favorite activity. Maybe it's playing guitar, coding your next iPhone app, fixing your motorcycle, or writing that novel. This activity, whenever you do it, pulls you in like a magnet. Your mind, body, and intuition are working in perfect harmony. You lose track of time. Why does it happen? Because you love with passion what you're doing! It means you're using one or more of your natural talents. Then ask yourself this question, "is it possible to capture the magic of a weekend and use it on your job during the week?" Of course, it is!

(iii) What do you long to do now?

What fire is burning inside of you at this very moment? What would you love to do for the rest of your life? If you know what it is, start doing it right now. Regardless of age or occupation, there is never a better time to start doing what you love, but now. Do you enjoy writing? Great. Start a blog. Does meeting and connecting with new people send you into happiness overdrive? Perfect. Launch a weekly meet-up for professional women in your town.

In an ideal world, everyone should use their natural talents at work every day. Unfortunately, that's not the case for most people. Studies show that more than 60 percent of workers are not entirely dedicated to their work.[48] While there may be multiple reasons for this, one of the key factors is that most workers don't get to use their natural talents at work daily.

The mission in life is not clear for everyone early in our lives. Only a few fortunate individuals sense it from their youth. Most of us need some years to pass and experience to be gained to identify it. And sadly, quite a few of us will not have even heard about it until the end of our lives.

REMEMBER: YOUR MISSION IN LIFE NEEDS TO
BE BASED ON YOUR GOD-GIVEN TALENTS

Finding the mission in life is one thing, and articulating it is another. The next chapter will teach us how to do that.

Moments of Reflection

1. What roles do you currently play on the stage of life? How are they going to change in the future?
2. What is personal leadership?
3. Review your visible and not so obvious talents; are you using them day by day?
4. What's the activity that gives you the most happiness?
5. Are you content at work? Are your strengths being used to full potential?
6. In solitude, ask yourself, "why am I on this earth?"
7. What's your mission in life? Why do you say so?

CHAPTER 10
MISSION STATEMENTS

—·◆·—

"Love does no wrong to a neighbor; therefore,
love is the fulfilling of the law."
(Romans 13:10)

I n this chapter, we're going to learn how to structure and articulate the
mission we have designed for ourselves, and how to make it the center
of our lives. But before we do that, let's look at the mission statement of
Oprah Winfrey, founder of The Oprah Winfrey TV network.[49]

*"To be a teacher. And to be known for inspiring my students to be more
than they thought they could be."*

Isn't it wonderful in its simplicity? In an issue of O magazine, Winfrey
recalls watching her grandmother make butter and wash clothes in a cast-
iron pot in the yard. A voice inside her told her life would be more than
hanging clothes on a line. She eventually realized she wanted to be a teacher,
but *"I never imagined it would be on TV,"* she writes.

A mission statement is a well-thought-out and considered articulation
of the reason for the existence of individuals, families, and organizations.

A mission statement is a formal written declaration of the core purpose and focus of the individual or group that generally remains unchanged over time. Suitably crafted mission statements serve as filters to separate what is essential from what is not, clearly state which areas of interest will be served, and communicate a sense of direction to the entire group. Like any critical foundational document, a mission statement must be proposed, debated, revised, and adopted by all interested parties, so they become "the living constitution" of that group.[50]

Personal Mission Statement

> "You therefore must be perfect, as your heavenly
> Father is perfect." (Matthews 5:48)

A personal mission statement is always the result of deep inner struggle and long soul-searching. It is a very intimate and private body of thoughts describing one's belief system and direction in life. It is an essential milestone in the developmental process of an individual, and a sure sign of maturity. Generally, a mission statement encapsulates the essence of a mature person, and it goes hand- in- hand with his or her character. However, this does not mean that younger people should not attempt to prepare their mission statements. On the contrary, Stepping Stone 3 is a call, an invitation, and a how-to addressed to people of all ages. The earlier you start in life to think about your mission, and the sooner you draft it, the better off you'll be in the future.

To be effective, the personal mission statement must be sincere, simple, and transparent. And it must be in writing. As such, it provides direction, consistency of action during long periods, and above all, becomes a solid anchor during stormy seasons of life. One should note, however, that statements change with time for the simple reason that the roles played in life change with time. For example, the mission statement of an older woman in her seventies for sure is different from her mission when she was active professionally, which in turn is unlike her mission when she was a young mother. Rewriting our mission statements should be a reflection of the transformation process that affects all of us during life's journey.

Mission statement of a father

Following is an example of a personal mission statement of a Christian father in the prime of his life:

"I am committed to living my life by Christian principles and teachings. I accept the will and guidance of the Lord Jesus Christ, God the Father, and the Holy Spirit. I believe in the sanctity of life and in upholding the sacred rights of my fellow countrymen. My foremost temporal duties are first toward myself, my family, and those who love us. Then, to my community and country. These are my current roles and goals in life:"

Roles	Goals
Myself as a Christian	Love the Lord God with all my heart, soul, and mind. Go to church regularly, assist fellow believers, take the Good News to the temporary world.
Myself as a human being	Take care of my body, mind, and spirit. Resolve to improve myself continually.
Head of the family	Provide leadership in all aspects of family life. Provide for the material, emotional, and spiritual wellbeing of my family. Offer guidance, assistance, and comfort to those who need it. Be the solid rock of the family during stormy times.
Husband	I love and respect my best friend and companion in life. Spend time with her, listen to her needs and advice, and assist her in all she does.

Father	Be a role model for my children. Love and respect them, discipline them when necessary. Teach them the same principles that guide me in life. Encourage them to become self-reliant and honorable people. Provide them with inspiration, encouragement, and assistance to pursue their educational goals.
Son and brother	Draw from the wisdom and experience of my parents. Stay close to, and assist them as necessary. Stay close to other members of the extended family. Participate in the preservation and continuation of family culture and traditions.
Businessman	Be genuinely committed to the well-being of my business, its associates, and employees. Always search for new ways to expand and improve what we're doing.
Benefactor	Always assist people in need. Make regular donations to my church and charity organizations of my choosing.
Citizen	Participate in accordance with my interests and best abilities to the community, civic, and political life of my country.

Mission statement of a young student

Following is a simplified version of a personal mission statement of a young female Christian student:

"I am committed to living my life under Christian principles and teachings. I accept the will and guidance of the Lord Jesus Christ, God the Father, and the Holy Spirit. These are my current roles and goals in life:"

Roles	Goals
Myself as a Christian	Love the Lord God with all my heart; attend church regularly, help fellow Christians

Myself as a human being and student	Take care of my body, mind, and spirit. Resolve to improve myself continually. Resolve to acquire as much knowledge in school as I can.
Daughter and sibling	Love and respect my parents, brothers, and all the other members of my family. Learn and respect family values and traditions.
Friend	Love and respect my friends, spend quality time with them, assist them in any way I can.

REMEMBER: A PERSONAL MISSION STATEMENT
PROVIDES DIRECTION AND PURPOSE IN LIFE

Family Mission Statement

Many families in our society are managed based on moods, circumstances, crises, quick fixes, and instant gratifications—not on sound principles. This is an unfortunate and awful situation. It is terrible because families become disjointed, aimless, and drifting apart, thus failing to fulfill one of their primary mission: family unity. Symptoms of a disorganized family surface whenever stress and pressure mount. People become angry, cynical, critical, uncooperative, and selfish. Disputes and fights erupt all the time, and simple verbal communications become yelling matches. Children who observe this kind of behavior grow up thinking the only way to solve problems with other people is to fight or flight. What a shame!

The core of a family should be what is changeless, what is always going to be there, namely, shared vision and values. By writing a family mission statement, you give expression to its real foundation. The mission statement

becomes a family's constitution, the standard, the criterion for evaluation, and decision making. When individual values align themselves with
those of the family, members work together for the common purpose they
intensely believe in.

A family mission statement must be based on Christian values and
follow the principles described in this chapter. When done collectively
and applied consistently, it becomes the unchanging core of the family, its
guiding light in life. It will take the family through good and bad times and
provide an unbreakable bond between members. However, it must reflect
the shared vision and values of everyone within the family, no matter how
old or young. For members to buy into the family mission statement, they
must be fully involved in its creation. This takes time, patience, involvement,
and skills. *"No involvement - no commitment"* is the law that many parents
forget when dealing with their children, mainly if they are younger.

The process of creating a family mission statement is as vital as the
result of the process--the mission statement itself. The very act of writing
and defining such a document becomes a key way to improve family life
and pull it together. Getting input from every member, drafting a statement, getting feedback, and using words offered by members in subsequent
revised versions are an uplifting process. It gets the family interacting with
vigor, communicating, and sharing thoughts on things that matter deeply
to them. The best statements are the result of members coming together in
a spirit of mutual respect and trust, expressing different views, and working collectively to create something greater than any one individual could
do alone. The mission statement becomes the framework for thinking, for
governing the family, and for resolving disputes. It creates the synergy in
the family that very few other activities can do.

REMEMBER: ALL FAMILY MEMBERS MUST
BE INVOLVED IN THE CREATION OF
THE FAMILY MISSION STATEMENT

The following is an outline of a mission statement of a Christian family with two young children:

"Our family is where we live our lives according to our Christian faith. It is where we pray together, grow together, and where we laugh together. It is the place where we belong. The family bonds us together during good times and bad times. Each member of the family is a unique individual with their own needs, desires, and aspirations. It is the family that offers the best environment for each of us to feel secure, grow, and have fun. We inherited family traditions from our parents and are committed to preserving and passing them over to younger generations.

Each member of our family deserves equal love, respect, and trust. We talk to each other calmly, with deference and consideration. When disputes arise, we solve them in the spirit of family, love, and trust. We do not fight, we do not scream, we do not berate each other. Younger members of the family seek advice and help from the older members. Older members of the family take care of the material, emotional, and spiritual well-being of the children.

For the family to function properly on a day-to-day basis, each member has duties and responsibilities. These duties and responsibilities are not imposed on anyone; they are the freewill expression of each member to participate in the family life. Also, the family establishes a daily routine that works efficiently for all. Regular schedule includes breakfast, school, homework time, extracurricular activities, time for play and sports, dinner time together, relaxation and devotion in the evening, and bedtime routine."

> REMEMBER: FAMILY MISSION STATEMENT
> KEEPS THE FAMILY UNITED IN COMMON
> VALUES AND PURPOSE.

Family Councils

Family councils are a very effective means of reinforcing or revisiting family mission statements at regular intervals. For families with children in school or college, they should take place twice a year, say at the beginning and ending of the school terms. For other families, one family council at the end of the calendar year may suffice.

Family councils may be called for special events, such as family plans to relocate or buy a new house. Also, when the father gets a promotion, or the mother expects to bring another member of the family to this world. Every member of the family, regardless of age, should have the right to call a family council, but the call should be seconded by another member, preferably by one of the adults.

Family councils are the perfect place for every member of the family to review his or her achievements, to disclose important plans, or to bring forth notable wishes, necessities, or problems. They keep the family informed about each other and increase the bonds of unity among them. Depending on the circumstances, family councils will also offer the ideal setting to review and update the mission statement of the family.

Organizational Mission Statements

Effective mission statements are also vital to organizations of any kind: nonprofit, religious, political, commercial, educational, and so on. To be effective, the statement must come from the insides of the organization, not from top managers, planners, or consultants. Everyone in it--irrespective of their position, professional knowledge, or salary level--should participate in a voluntary and meaningful way to the drafting and adopting the mission statement.

Religious Organizations

Every religious organization, no matter how small or large, should have a meaningful mission statement to act as their constitution. The guiding light for it should be Jesus's calling to all Christians when he told them: "You shall love the Lord your God with all your heart and with all your soul and with all your mind." (Matthew 22:37)

> **Train up a child**
> **in the way he should go:**
> **and when he is old,**
> **he will not depart from it.**
> **Proverbs 22:6**

Starting from this commandment, here is an example of a mission statement for a small worship and charity group:

"The mission of our group is to lead people into a growing relationship with Jesus Christ. We accomplish our mission by creating environments where people are encouraged and equipped to pursue intimacy with God.

Besides weekly gatherings to praise the Lord, we organize Bible study classes, youth clubs, and recreational activities. We also offer personalized counseling to people who need emotional and spiritual help.

We focus our charitable work to helping the homeless in our community. We do this by conducting fundraising activities on our own or in collaboration with sister organizations.

Our staff consists of dedicated volunteers and qualified spiritual leaders with experience relevant to the needs of our group."

> REMEMBER: ORGANIZATIONAL
> MISSION STATEMENT
> CREATES GREAT UNITY AND
> TREMENDOUS COMMITMENT
> AMONG ITS STAKEHOLDERS

Ready to move on to the next chapter? If you thought you knew how to do long-term planning, such as building wealth, your know-how would be much enhanced by the principles outlined in the next chapter titled *Long Term Planning*.

Moments of Reflection

1. What are mission statements? Why are they important?
2. Think and draft your mission statement; review it after a few days and finalize it. Review it at least once a year.
3. Gather your family together and spend time discussing the purpose and values of family life. Introduce to them the concept of the mission statement
4. Prepare the first draft of your family mission statement and review it with its members. Debate and adopt the final version.
5. Print and frame the family mission statement and display it for all to see.

6. What would make an excellent opportunity for you to call a family council during the next six months?

7. If you belong to a Christian group, take the initiative to draft a mission statement for it.

CHAPTER 11
LONG-TERM PLANNING

—◦◦◦◆◦◦◦—

"Of old you laid the foundation of the earth, and
the heavens are the work of your hands. They will
perish, but you will remain." (Psalm 102:25-27)

Three Kernels of Corn – A Story About Long-Term Thinking[51]

Three young men were once given three kernels of corn apiece by a wise, old sage who encouraged them to go out into the world and use the corn to bring themselves good fortune.

The first young man immediately put his three kernels of corn into a bowl of hot broth and ate them.

The second thought, *"I can do better than that,"* and he planted his three kernels of corn. Within a few months, he had three stalks of corn. He took the ears of corn from the stems, boiled them, and had enough corn for three meals.

The third man said to himself, *"I can do better than that!"* He also planted his three kernels of corn, but when his three stalks of corn produced, he stripped one of the stems and replanted all of the seeds in it, he gave the second stalk of corn to a sweet maiden, and he ate the third.

His replanted corn kernels gave him 200 stalks of corn! And the seeds of these he continued to replant, setting aside only a bare minimum to eat. He eventually planted a hundred acres of corn. With his fortune, he not only won the hand of the sweet maiden but purchased the land owned by the sweet maiden's father. And he and his family were never hungry again."

This old parable is an excellent reminder that it's not what we have that matters; it's what we do with it. We can waste the opportunities given to us or make a plan that will enable our success in the long-term.

In this chapter, we will address the issue of Long-Term Planning, which is the first stage of the principle of double creation. Long-term planning is essential in all aspects of our life, starting from simple things like yearly vacations, to more complex issues such as professional career or financial security.

The First Mental Creation

In one of the previous chapters, we were introduced to the principle of Double Creation, which states that all things are created twice. There is first, a mental creation, followed by second, a physical creation. The first creation is virtual; the second is in reality. Let's now drill a bit deeper into this principle, with a focus on the virtual creation related to various aspects of modern life.

The first creation is the result of a planning process. It takes you along the imaginary road you want to travel before you start your journey. The first creation simply tells you to begin with a clear understanding of your destination. It requires you to know where you are right now and where you're going so that the steps you take are always in the right direction. The principle of double creation applies to all aspects of our life, such as work, school, career, retirement, and so on. It is important to work hard, but it is vital to work smart. Working smart means acting by a well-thought-out plan. Be aware that it is incredibly easy to get caught in the activity trap, in the rat race of life, to work harder and harder at climbing the ladder of success, only to discover that it leans against the wrong wall! When you reach the top of the ladder, you realize that your goal was either ephemeral or not right for you. Unfortunately, it is possible to be very, very busy without getting anywhere!

People often find themselves achieving empty victories, successes that have come at the expense of things they realize are far more valuable to them. People from every walk of life, such as politicians, plumbers, teachers, and business-people often struggle to achieve a higher income, higher recognition, and better social status, only to find out their drive to succeed has blinded them to the things that mattered most. And what matters most? For many people, it is the family, peace of mind, connection to the Almighty, or their health. And now, once you realize you were chasing the wrong goals, it's too late, because those things that matter most might be gone forever.

Let's look at parenting as a long-term planning exercise. It is apparent that we need long-term thinking because kids will grow up, they need to go to school, will require funds for higher education, will get married, and so on. The earlier you accept the necessity for long-term planning, the easier it will be to prepare for the upcoming events. The same is true with your own biological life: you know that eventually, you will grow old, that retirement years are coming, that you need to prepare for old age when you need help. Wise people think very long- term, not only with their lives, but with the lives of their children and even that of their grandchildren.

> ## REMEMBER: LONG-TERM PLANNING IS THE CRITICAL COMPONENT OF THE FIRST CREATION

Wealth Building

<u>What Is Wealth?</u>

Money, riches, wealth - we humans are all fascinated by these words, by the glamor, excitement, and promise of happiness they entail. It is in our instincts to judge someone for the wealth they inherit or accumulate during a lifetime. We either admire or envy those people; there is no middle judgment. It is a reality that money-making, riches, and wealth have been part of human civilization since biblical times, and most likely will be so for many centuries to come.

We all know what money is, but what are riches? What is wealth? Webster's dictionary defines riches as *"things that make one rich,"* and wealth, as the *"abundance of valuable material possessions or resources."*[52]

The biblical frame of reference for wealth is that God is the source of all gain. It is he who owns everything, and just entrusts some of us to manage it while on the earth. We are mere stewards of whatever God gives us, including wealth. God is, therefore, not opposed to wealth since it comes from Him. Many prominent Bible characters such as Abraham, Job, Joseph, Solomon and David are quite well-to-do people. God is not opposed to wealth and money, but he definitely is against the love of money.

> **But thou shalt remember**
> **the LORD thy God: for it is he**
> **that giveth thee power to get wealth...**
> **Deuteronomy 8:18**

Since all wealth flows from the loving provisions of God, our role is to be sensible, faithful stewards of it. If God designates us as caretakers of his assets, we must be very humble in accepting it. Therefore, what matters most is not how much we possess, but how we use that which is entrusted to us. At the end of your life on earth, you will be evaluated on how well you handled what God entrusted to you, including money. Most people fail to realize that money is both a test and a trust from God. God uses finances to teach us to trust him and watches us how trustworthy we are. Let's remember that the more God gives you, the more responsible he expects you to be.

Jesus often referred to life as a trust and told stories to illustrate this responsibility towards God. The parable of the talents tells about a businessman who must go away for some time. He entrusts his wealth to the care of his servants. One servant receives five talents, another two, and the third just one. When the master returns, he evaluates each servant's performance records and rewards them accordingly. The first one who doubled his money by trading is rewarded with praise and promotion; the second one who doubled the money in other ways is also praised and promoted; but the third one, who hid the one talent in the earth because of fear of losing it, the master punished. And Jesus concludes by saying: "For unto every one that has it shall be given, and he shall have abundance; but from him that has not, it shall be taken away even that which he has." (Matthew 25:29)

The above statement made by Jesus may be shocking to many people because it appears to uphold and increase inequality between men. But Jesus is merely stating what is deeply ingrained in human society since its creation: God wants good performance rewarded, and lack of it penalized.

To conclude this section, let's use secular vocabulary to define wealth: Wealth is material possessions acquired ethically and managed according to the highest moral code. That means money should not only be gained legally, but ethically as well. Managing the cash implies that after we cover our living expenses, we diligently save, invest, and take care of others too.

> REMEMBER: WEALTH IS MONEY
> ACQUIRED ETHICALLY
> AND MANAGED ACCORDING TO
> A HIGH MORAL CODE

How to Build Wealth

Before asking ourselves how to build wealth, we must raise the question, *"why build it in the first place"?* From a Christian perspective, the answer should come in two parts: (a) *"because God is allowing me to do it"* and (b) *"because wealth gives us the power to do good deeds in life."*

Wealth building is a long-term proposition that requires skills, a robust set of moral values, and above all, discipline. Wealth cannot be purchased; it can only be built.[53] Wealth does not come to everyone; it comes most to those who are prepared for it. And it does not come easy. Some people may get a temporary windfall of cash, such as an inheritance, lucky trade on Wall Street, or lottery win, and think they are wealthy. Only to find out they are not ready for it, watching how their unexpected fortune evaporates in a blink of an eye the same way it arrived. So, to build wealth, one has to start early, acquire necessary financial know-how from youth, seek specialized advice when needed, and run his/her finances cool-headed and with an iron hand.

What are the critical tasks you should focus on when improving the state of your current finances? Follow these common-sense rules:

- Spend no more than 30 percent of income on housing.
- Keep three months of living expenses in an emergency saving account.
- Save at least 10 percent of monthly income.
- Carry adequate life and healthcare insurance all the time.

- Take advantage of the company match for your 401k retirement savings account.
- Make maximum contribution to your Roth IRA individual retirement account.
- Open a college savings account for your children.
- Seek professional advice to optimize tax liabilities.
- Let professionals manage your retirement portfolio.

I am Becoming Wealthy. Now What?

Now that you are becoming wealthy, what do you do? How do you start using your wealth? Again, if you keep in mind that you are just a steward of God's riches, then answers should come quickly: provide a legacy of giving, humility, and gratitude; support noble and worthy causes dear to your heart. Priorities should be distinct: (a) your family endowment first (b) your church and community (c) your country.

America has a long and proud tradition of generosity, benevolence, and promoting the welfare of others. There are plenty of well-known philanthropic organizations such as the Henry Ford Foundation, Rockefeller Foundation, Milton S. Hershey Trust, Melinda and Bill Gates Foundation, Warren Buffet Foundation, and so on. They were all started by outstanding citizens who knew how to build wealth for themselves, their families, and their fellow countrymen. Of course, there are thousands and thousands of more men or women of charity. Their names are etched on countless of churches, universities, colleges, libraries, schools, arts centers, public buildings, and spaces in memory of their generosity. You don't have to wait to become a millionaire to give. Start building your legacy today by providing every week whatever you can afford to your church, school, sports team, favorite charity, and even your neighborhood soup kitchen.

REMEMBER: WEALTH BUIDING IS A MARATHON,
NOT A SPRINT!

Money Management

The first prerequisite toward acquiring wealth is the ability to make and manage money. For most people, the salary or wages constitute the primary source of income, and monthly living costs are the most significant expenditure. The difference between income and expenses is called budgetary surplus or discretionary funds. The larger the surplus, the better your capacity for saving and investing. Given a fixed income, the art of managing money is to minimize the expenses and to grow the surplus.

The key to managing money is to learn how to live within your means. If you figure out how to live and save on a small income, then you will know how to manage more substantial amounts of cash when your time comes. Otherwise, money management can be a tricky, even deadly business. Start saving when you are young, make it a habit when your cash flow is weak, and do not wait for better cashflows. Make a monthly family budget now and stick to it. Show the benefits of saving to your family members and have them save with a worthy goal in mind. Teach young children the skills of making money, and the discipline of saving it. Do not borrow money for daily living or to buy stuff but do borrow it for purchasing assets. Pay off debts as fast as you can, particularly those that are consumer-related. Always focus on paying off higher-interest loans. Have a long-term plan to increase your net worth, which is the value of your assets less your liabilities. At the end of each year, check out your net worth. Celebrate when it is going up and ponder over it when it is stagnant or slides downward. Take corrective actions as required.

For regular families, other sources of income besides full-time daily jobs can be evening jobs, free-lancing, a small home-based business, capital gains from assets transactions, or dividends from investments. Make as much money as you can without overworking yourself and your family. There are times when families must undertake coordinated and sustained efforts to generate more money while living on a tight budget. For instance, when a family is saving for the down payment of their first house, or when a young couple is saving for going to college. But do not forget that periods of austerity and intense focusing will not last forever and must be balanced by a healthy family life during those times. And, at the end of it, by sweet rewards and celebrations!

> REMEMBER: THE GOLDEN RULE OF MONEY MANAGEMENT IS TO SPEND LESS THAN YOU MAKE

Let's turn the page now to see the conclusion and benefits of what we have learned while climbing toward Stepping Stone 3.

Moments of Reflection

1. Give examples of a lack of long-term planning in your life so far.
2. What are your top three long-term plans now?
3. Do you want to become wealthy? Why?
4. Where does wealth come from?
5. State the golden rule of money management.
6. Set up a family strategic plan for wealth building spanning two generations.

CHAPTER 12
THIS IS YOUR DESTINY

—◆•◆—

"Commit your work to the Lord, and your
plans will be established." (Proverbs 16:3)

This chapter will introduce you to the concept of destiny from a Christian perspective. You will see that contrary to secular culture, which looks at destiny as an evil blind force, the Christian view is that destiny is the actual realization of God's plans for each of us. However, this happens only if we, as people of free will, make the right choices in life and know how to read God's messages to us. You will also learn about the irrefutable link between the moral character of a person and his or her destiny. In a sense, your destiny is nothing but fulfilling your calling in life given to you by your Creator.

"Your destiny is the customized life calling God has ordained and equipped you to accomplish in order to bring Him the greatest glory and achieve the maximum expansion of His kingdom." Dr. Tony Evans[54]

What Is Destiny?

Destiny, fate, and fortune are words used in the temporal world to describe events beyond human control and which are not well understood. They are as old as civilization and had been used extensively in philosophy and literature.

What is destiny? To this inquiry, Webster's offers several definitions[55]:

- A predetermined course of events often held to be an irresistible power or agency.
- Something to which a person or thing is destined.

And what is fate? An inevitable and often adverse outcome, condition or end.

Even though these are definitely secular definitions, we cannot fail to notice that the irresistible power refers to God. For us believers, it is manifest that God has ordained our destiny because we are his children. He has also prescribed a plan for each of us from the very beginning. But most worldly people nowadays do not think about life in these terms, and do not understand the deep sense of destiny or fate. Those who do, perceive their destiny in a fatalistic and cynical way, as a set of events out in the future that cannot be stopped or avoided.

Although fate and destiny are considered synonyms in the contemporary English language, from a philosophical perspective, they are slightly different. Fate is regarded as an inevitable outcome, while destiny evokes some kind of a journey toward a destination. Fate is that you cannot change. Destiny is that you're meant to shape. Fate is what happens when you don't take responsibility for your life. Destiny is what happens when you commit to growing, learning, taking chances, and being in charge.[56] Fate is what happens to reactive people. Destiny is what the life of proactive people becomes.

Philosophy on destiny existed since ancient times. For instance, Socrates (470-399 BC), the stoic Greek philosopher, believed that human decisions and actions ultimately went according to a heavenly plan devised by the supreme god Zeus. Stoics claimed that although humans theoretically have free will, their souls and the circumstances under which they lived are all part of the universal network of fate. Secular literature on fate existed since ancient times and had a significant influence on the development of Western civilization. It consisted of legends and stories teaching the futility of trying to escape a cruel fate that has been correctly predicted. Classical Greek works include Sophocles's Oedipus Rex and Homer's Iliad and Odyssey. In England, fate played a notable literary role in Shakespeare's Macbeth (1606), Thomas Hardy's Tess of the d'Urbervilles (1891), and Samuel Beckett's Endgame (1957).

Character and Destiny

"It is your character, and your character alone, that will make your life happy or unhappy. That is all that really passes for destiny. And you choose it. No one else can give it to you or deny it to you. No rival can steal it from you. And no friend can give it to you. Others can encourage you to make the right choices or discourage you. But you choose."

The above words are found in the late Senator John McCain's (1936-2018) inspiring book on the link between character and destiny.[57] Many other thinkers share this view. As early as about two and a half millennia ago, the Greek philosopher Heraclitus (535-476 BC) told his fellow men that *"character is destiny"*[58]. In contrast, Aristoteles (384-322 BC) described virtues as being habits we acquire by *performing* virtuous actions. The French aristocrat Alexis de Tocqueville,[59] visiting America in 1835, wrote: *"America is great because she is good, but if America ever ceases to be good, she will cease to be great."* Much later, President Theodore Roosevelt (1860-1940) told us, *"character, in the long run, is the decisive factor in the life of an individual and of nations alike."*[60]

To further understand the connection of character to destiny, let's recall the poem attributed the Scottish author and government reformer Samuel Smiles (1812-1904) linking thoughts and habits to character, and character to destiny[61]:

> *"Sow a thought, reap an action*
> *Sow an action, reap a habit*
> *Sow a habit, reap a character,*
> *Sow a character, reap a destiny."*

This is precisely what this book teaches: the destiny of an individual will, in considerable measure, be influenced by his or her moral character. Therefore, by working on improving our integrity, we significantly increase the chances of building the future we aspire to have. Of course, all this is under the guidance and supervision of the Holy Spirit, as we shall see further down. The same thinking applies to our nation: American destiny is strongly affected by its character, which in turn is the sum of the characters of its individual citizens.

Unfortunately, we all recognize that our country is currently undergoing a major crisis of character that is threatening to destroy the very foundation of America the Good. Today, in the U.S., there are far too many kids pushing drugs, teenage girls having babies, 16-year-olds killing each other, and young people of all ages, races, and social backgrounds admitting to lying, cheating, and stealing. America will lose its prominence if we continue to graduate young people who are brilliant but dishonest, who have vast academic knowledge but don't care about others or have highly creative minds but are irresponsible. This self-destruction must stop as soon as possible. Character without knowledge is weak and irrelevant, but knowledge without integrity is dangerous and a potential menace to society. The destiny of America will be redressed only if we teach future generations to do what is right, to tell the truth, work hard, help their neighbor, face adversities with courage, and be undeterred in defeat and gracious in victory. And above all, to believe in God. This is what the soul of a nation is all about.

REMEMBER: YOUR MORAL CHARACTER AND
DESTINY ARE LINKED TO EACH OTHER

Your Christian Destiny

Do you possess a deep sense of personal destiny? Do you have the uplifting feeling that calls you to do something special? Did you notice that people who own a strong personal sense of calling or destiny are more influential individuals? Such people are relentless in pursuing their goals and dreams; they never give up. They have the character quality of perseverance that drives them to greatness in both a heavenly and an earthly sense. In other words, they have developed a Christ-like character.

The primary purpose of this book is to help believers develop their character and fulfill their calling. Now, to achieve a calling, one must hear it, understand it, and commit to it. The calling comes from God, who designed it specifically for you according to his predetermined plans for your life. The intercessor between you and God is the Holy Spirit, who lives in you, and who will help you interpret what God's message for you is all about. Therefore, your God-ordained plans make your Christian destiny.

An excellent way to understand Christian destiny is to look at the Apostle Paul's life. Paul states in Ephesians 3:7: "of which I was made a minister, according to the gift of God's grace which was given to me according to the working of his power." In other words, Paul did not make himself an apostle; he was appointed; he did not have any powers; he received them from God's grace. Paul was just obedient in fulfilling God's calling for his life.

What can we learn from Paul's life and his pre-ordained destiny? According to Pastor Drollinger,[62] there are several necessary steps in fulfilling one's Christian destiny:

(i) Determine and affirm your calling: Whether you are a student, a homemaker mother, an executive, laborer, or office worker, you must first determine and affirm your calling. Did you select your vocation and attain your position by your power, or did Christ appoint you? God made the Apostle Paul a servant/minister; he did not appoint himself. The same is right for you. If what you do is your calling, keep doing it because this is how you please God. Do it well, do it with passion, and do it with humility. If what you're doing now is not your calling, keep talking to God to guide you, then change your job by his plans.

(ii) Cementing your calling: For those who possess a legitimate call by God to serve in various capacities, they will want to figure out and cement what exactly has God called them out to do. For instance, if you feel your calling is serving in the military, you must drill deeper into figuring out what exactly it entails from a practical viewpoint. But never lose your sense of servanthood, and never let things that in the world's eyes are of supreme value--i.e., prestige, reputation, success--take over your mind. When you do that, you diminish your spiritual power, moral authority, and effectiveness.

(iii) Fulfill your calling: Whatever you do, do it well, do it with passion, and do it cheerfully. And always remain humble. You are watched by many eyes who want to see how you perform. Some may wish you ill, but most will look at you with admiration and respect. Your moral authority speaks louder than anything else. Thus, you become a role model for people around you.

(iv) Fuel your calling: The fuel for fulfilling your calling is God's tremendous power working through you. This fuel is never-ending; it can simply be replenished by praying and talking with God.

> REMEMBER: YOUR CHRISTIAN DESTINY
> IS TO FULFILL GOD'S PRE-ORDAINED
> PLANS FOR YOUR LIFE

An Extraordinary Life

Do you want to live a life that is out of the ordinary? An entity that is way beyond mere existence, survival, boredom, and grinding routines? An experience in which you can look forward to every day with optimism and excitement? A life in which everything that comes to you is stimulating, enlightening, and rewarding? Do you want your children to say to you many years from now: "Mom, you are such a special mother, and your life has been so extraordinary!"

**The difference between
ordinary and extraordinary is a
little bit of 'extra' done every day.
Anthony Robins**

Then look no further. As a proactive Christian, your life will be extraordinary because you are destined to make it as such. Once you build your Diamond Soul character, it, in turn, will help you fulfill your destiny under God's grace. Make your life as unique as you are. Do not fear extraordinary––embrace it! Take the road less traveled and take delight in discovering new vistas! Shoot for the stars, live with passion, and enjoy every moment of it! Why? Because this is what God wants you to do!

"You make known to me the path of life; in your presence there is fullness of joy; at your right hand are pleasures forevermore. (Psalm 16:11)"

> REMEMBER: YOUR DIAMOND SOUL
> CHARACTER WILL OFFER YOU AN
> EXTRAORDINARY LIFE TO ENJOY!

Standing on Stepping Stone 3: Your Godly Way

Christian virtues of hope, perseverance, and patience are at the foundation of Stepping Stone 3. Based on it, you use the principle of double creation to plan our life in its totality. The key is to detect God's plans for you and design the details of your life around them. You can only be successful if you continuously consult with the Holy Spirit, who resides inside your being. Your life as a believer is a collaboration project between the Holy Spirit and you. Holy Spirit provides guidance, and you provide muscle power. To put it differently, the Holy Spirit brings hope to the table while you bring perseverance and patience.

Stepping Stone 3 also represents the critical habit of personal leadership. According to it, from this point on, your life will not just happen haphazardly. Your efforts to fulfill God's purpose will mold it. Under the guidance of the Holy Spirit, you will look for the meaning and mission of life and visualize your path. Your direction in life will be accompanied by a set of moral values guiding you during quiet and stormy times as well. This is what you will call your godly way.

Now as you stand proudly on Stepping Stone 3, let's look together at what you should do from this point on:

- Think strategically way ahead in the future: months, quarters, years, decades, even one or two generations.
- Define the major roles you play in different stages of your life.
- Define clear goals and objectives in each role and set out to achieve them.
- Use personal leadership skills to trace a clear path for your future.
- Search for your mission and meaning in life.
- Write your personal mission statement.
- Champion the process of creating mission statements for your family and other groups.
- Build sustainable well-being, security, and wealth for your family.
- Leave a legacy of giving, service, and humility.
- As you build your Diamond Soul character over the years, watch it shape your God-given destiny.
- Be prepared to live and enjoy the extraordinary life that God has prepared for you.

"Build your Christlike Diamond Character first, then watch your God-ordained destiny unfolds before your very eyes."

Dear reader, you have attained an important milestone on your way up: there are only two more Stepping Stones between you and the summit you want to reach. The next one is Stepping Stone 4, *I am Disciplined*, and the last one is Stepping Stone 5, *Polishing your Character*. Let's turn the page together to learn new and exciting things!

Moments of Reflection

1. What is Destiny?

2. How is Destiny related to Character?

3. Meditate about your destiny do far: Can you perceive it? Are you happy with it? Do you want to change it?

4. Why live an extraordinary life? Does this scare you?

5. List and meditate about Christian virtues associated with Stepping Stone 3. How do you practice them every day?

6. Now that you have reached Stepping Stone 3, how did your thinking change? Which are the new paradigms you have gained about life? Why are they better than the previous ones?

YOU ARE DISCIPLINED

—◆•◆•◆—

Virtues: Temperance, Diligence

"And every man that striveth for the mastery is temperate in all things." (1 Corinthians 9:25)

CHAPTER 13
THE MYSTERY OF TIME

━━◆◆●◆◆━━

"In the beginning, God created the heaven
and the earth." (Genesis 1:1)

S tepping Stone 4 is the platform on which we learn about the principles of exercising willpower, personal discipline, and personal management. It represents the Christian virtues of Temperance and Diligence. Stepping Stone 4 is also called the platform of personal management because it gives us the managerial know-how for organizing and executing the necessary plans to reach our personal goals.

We can reach Stepping Stone 4 only coming from the previous one, which is the platform of personal leadership. We must first have a plan to execute before we use the necessary tools for its implementation. The plan is the path in life––established on platform Stepping Stone 3––and the means for its application are found on platform Stepping Stone 4. As we were guided by the Holy Spirit on all previous platforms, so on this one we need his continuous divine presence, guidance, and encouragement. Being self-disciplined all the time is a mighty task, and most people who attempt to acquire this skill on their own are doomed to failure. But with the cooperation of the Holy Spirit, I can assure you it becomes possible.

This chapter discusses the concept of time and its significance in our daily life. Equally critical, it analyses the difference between the words important and urgent as applied to tasks and priorities.

What Is Time?

Let me start with a story[63]:

A long time ago a man was very successful and had gathered a lot of wealth. Everybody respected him, and he was a source of inspiration. When he was taking his last breathes, all the members of the family were around him.

One of his sons said, *"Dad, please give us some valuable lessons from your life.»*

The dying man said, *"I will give you a lesson, but for that I require some more time. As you can see, I am running out of it. Please take all my wealth and buy some extra time for me."*

The son, puzzled by his father's odd request, replied, *"Dad, it is not possible to buy time even if we have all the money the world."*

The father said, *"Yes, my son, you're so right, time cannot be bought. So, this is my life lesson to you: time is free of cost, but it's limited and cannot be accumulated. Hence, time is priceless. Make the best use of it as you can."*

Time is still a mystery for us humans. Despite many definitions provided by scientists, philosophers, and engineers, the secular world still does not understand exactly what time is. Fortunately for us Christians, we can rely on the biblical perspective of time as the one of significance because it comes directly from God. Let's review now quickly what time means to God and different groups of learned people.

God's Time

Time is the creation of the eternal God. God always has been and will forever be, because God dwells in eternity. Scripture says that after God made the heavens and earth, he also brought into being the day and night.

Regarding us humans, this is what the Scriptures teach us:

- That human time is different from God's time: ""But, beloved, be not ignorant of this one thing, that one day *is* with the Lord as a thousand years, and a thousand years as one day. (2 Peter 3:8)

- While on this earth, we are also told to use our time wisely. "Walk in wisdom toward them that are without, redeeming the time." (Colossians 4:5)

- That future times are known only by God: "But of that day and *that* hour knoweth no man, no, not the angels which are in heaven, neither the Son, but the Father." (Mark 13:32)

Concerning the Christian perspective on time, it is worth bringing up a most surprising, yet proper definition of time provided by Pastor Rick Warren: *"time is best expression of love."*[64] How can this be? Simply because the essence of love is not what we think or do for others, but how much we give of ourselves to others. The most desired gifts of love are not diamonds, or roses or chocolate; it is focused attention. Focused attention says, *"I value you enough to give you my most precious asset--my time."*

Scientist's Time

Time is something we deal with every day and something that everyone thinks they understand. However, there is no one single and straightforward definition of time[65]. Short descriptions include 'what clock measures,' and 'a certain period during which something is done.' Others, more elaborate, state that time is 'a dimension of the physical universe that orders the sequence of events at a given place.'

What's the current scientific understanding of time? Scientists will tell you that time started way back in the past during the Big Bang explosion, which created the universe about 13.7 billion years ago, but it will go indefinitely in the future. In other words, time has a sure start but no end in sight. Which begs the question: "Before Big Bang, was time present even if the universe did not exist?" And, to make the matter even more interesting, Albert Einstein's theory of relativity postulates that time is flexible; it will compress or stretch depending on the speed of the object you observe and the speed of the observer.[66] Wow! How can this be? Wait! There is more: Modern astrophysics theories tell us to regard time, not as a separate entity, but connected to space, into a so-called "time-space" indivisible construct. Hmm...Don't worry if you're confused; you're not alone!

Philosopher's Time

Unlike scientist's time, philosophy of space and time is the branch of philosophy concerned with the issues surrounding the existence and character of space and time. The subject focuses on several fundamental topics, such as if time and space exist outside of the mind and whether they exist independently of one another.

In ancient Greek mythology, the personification of time was Chronos, depicted as an immortal, old, wise man with wings. According to the legend, Chronos was conceived by Earth and Water, and he, in turn, created the first generation of gods. In modern English, his name is used in words related to the passage of time, such as chronicles, chronograph, and chronometer. Later on, the great Greek thinker Plato (427-347 BC) identifies time with the period of motion of heavenly bodies.[67]

In early Christianity, Saint Augustine of Hippo (344-430) contemplates the nature of time, asking, *"What then is time? If no one asks me, I know: if I wish to explain it to one that asked, I know not."*[68] During the Age of Reason, two intellectual giants, Isaac Newton (1643-1727) and Gottfried

Leibniz (1646-1716), debated the issue of time with wit and humor to the delight of their contemporaries.

Engineer's Time

The early man estimated passage of time by observing repeating events in the skies such as moving of the sun, moon, and stars. Besides, he also watched regular occurrences on earth like seasonal rains, the flowering of trees and plants, and so on. Pretty soon, he started keeping records of what he saw, thus giving birth to calendars and the science of astronomy. The Chinese and Babylonians were among the first to divide the year into 12 months and each month into 30 days.

The first human-made object designed to tell time was the sundial, based on the movement of a shadow of a tall object on the ground during a sunny day. This was the first clock. Later on, inventions were made to divide the day or the night into different periods to regulate work or rituals. For instance, night oil lamps or wax candles were marked to tell the passage of time. Such divisions became known as hours, but they did not have a fixed length until the ancient Greeks divided the day equally into 24 hours.

Hourglasses, also known as sandglasses or clepsydras, were used in Renaissance Europe to measure specific periods and determine the duration of church sermons, university lectures, and even sessions of torture. Mechanical clocks replaced the old sandglasses starting in the 13th century, and elaborate clocks were built in public places such as city towers and churches. The use of the pendulum mechanism significantly improved the accuracy of timepieces. Pendulum clocks, known nowadays as Grandfather clocks, quickly became a household item with well-to-do European and American families. In 1761, the British Navy commissioned John Harrison to build a high-accuracy maritime clock to determine the longitude of a ship on high seas.[69]

The modern standard on measuring time on a global scale was established at a conference in England in 1884 and became known as the GMT (Greenwich Mean Time) standard.[70] Nowadays, we measure time accurately by using atomic clocks based on the fixed rate of change of electron transition frequency. All high-tech devices, such as computers, smartphones, and GPS's use some sort of high-accuracy wave signal generators and time measurement chips.

REMEMBER: GOD HAS CREATED
TIME AND ETERNITY.
GOD'S TIME IS DIFFERENT THAN OURS

Time Shortage

So, what is time? Unfortunately, none of the scientific or philosophical definitions provide a useful answer for our daily lives. Clearly, time is not an object or substance we can touch or see, but neither is merely a dimension, quantity, or a concept. From a practical perspective, time is pervasive in our lives, has many aspects, and appears to represent different things to different people. Consider these phrases: "time stood still," "it's time for dinner," "adolescence is a difficult time," and so on. In this chapter, we will discuss how time relates to our daily lives.

We all learn in school that a year has 365 days, a day 24 hours, an hour 60 minutes, and a minute 60 seconds. During a 24-hour day, we sleep about 8 hours, and are awake during the rest of the time. We also know that time is in short supply, as we always need more time to finish something or are on the run to be on time somewhere. Indeed, time flies too fast and is still in short supply. Therefore, time has value.

The phrase "time shortage" aptly depicts the dilemma of the Information Age: there is never enough time, life is too fast-paced, days are too hectic, and too much information floods us from all directions. We feel there are too many things to do, and there are too many distractions preventing us from doing them. Just consider how in the world a mother can squeeze in one day these many activities: going to work, shopping, keeping the household, cooking, and feeding the kids, helping with home-work, talking with her husband, driving the girls to soccer and ballet, and preparing for tomorrow––and be sane at the end of the day? And doing all this, while a ton of emails, messages, Instagrams, and Tweets flood her smartphone, screaming for her attention? If her grandparents were alive to see her coping with all this, they would say the society has gone mad. They wouldn't be too far from the truth, would they?

No wonder most of us share the feeling that life is out of control, that events are overwhelming us, and the most important things get lost in the daily fast-paced rat-race. Then the question becomes, 'how do we slow down the time,' or 'how do we manage ourselves better?'

REMEMBER: TIME IS YOUR MOST VALUABLE ASSET,
USE IT WISELY!

Time Management

Imagine life without time pressure, without a constant sense that you're running behind, frustrated that yet again, you're losing the battle against the irresistible force of the ticking clock. Life without time happens when you're involved in a pleasurable, leisurely activity, such as walking in the woods or sun-bathing on the beach. Isn't it a wonderful time spent without the tyranny of the clock?

> **Lost time is**
> **never found again.**
> **Benjamin Franklin**

Unfortunately, when we get back, we turn again in cogs and wheels in a giant machinery that moves continuously, without pause or breakdown. But it shouldn't be this way. In fact, human society has not always been obsessed with time. Before the Industrial Revolution, clocks were mostly irrelevant. Instead of focusing on time, people concentrated on their tasks. Most of them were peasants, so they worked in the natural order, at the right time. What about us going back to the principle of task orientation, without the pressure of time? That would be wonderful, wouldn't it? Read further down to learn how to move from a paradigm of time management to one of task management. But for us to undertake this transition, it is useful to look briefly at how the idea of time management has evolved over the years.

Time management is a relatively new concept that appeared during the First Industrial Revolution about three centuries ago. Its purpose was to help synchronize the work of laborers involved in the manufacturing processes and other types of disciplined activities such as those in the military, public education, governmental bodies, hospitals, etc. Time management soon moved from groups to individuals, to help them sort out, organize, and prioritize daily or weekly activities.

The current definition of time management is 'the process of planning and exercising conscious control of time spent on specific activities, especially to increase effectiveness, efficiency, or productivity.'[71] This definition applies mostly to industrial manufacturing processes, where lots of people must do individual tasks in a synchronized manner. The same goals of increasing productivity can be successfully applied to personal activities. In this case, the time management is called personal time management. The remaining question then becomes, 'how do we do it?'

A glimpse back in time will instruct us that there have been three major approaches to personal time management, each building and improving on the previous one, and each moving us to control our lives better. Let's look at each of them quickly.

The first approach was characterized by notes and to-do-lists. Task lists have been a significant leap from the prior "no list at all" environment, but they took much time to maintain.

The second approach was defined by calendars, schedulers, and appointment books—new tools reflecting an attempt to look ahead and to schedule events and activities in the future. Although very much in use today, the second approach fails to address the issue of importance and urgency of tasks, and the resulting necessity for prioritization.

The third generation reflects the contemporary body of knowledge about managing time. It adds to those preceding attempts the idea of prioritization based on the critical concepts of essential and urgent. Moreover, it requires establishing the value of each activity and setting long-term goals and short-term objectives towards which energy should be directed.

A critical milestone in the quest for prioritization was the introduction of the Eisenhower matrix. The matrix is a simple yet effective method of categorizing tasks according to their importance or urgency, thus helping a lot in the decision-making process. Years ago, when President Eisenhower (1890-1969) was asked what problems he faced on a daily basis, he replied:

"I have two kinds of problems, the urgent and the important. What both-
ers me is that the urgent are not important, and the important are never
urgent."[72] This method of classification was used by the U.S. military during
the Second World War and was very much liked by the Supreme Allied
Commander in Europe, General Eisenhower.

According to the Eisenhower Method,[73] tasks are evaluated using the
criteria important/unimportant and urgent/not urgent, and then placed
in matching quadrants in a four-quadrant matrix. Jobs are then handled
as follows:

1. Important/Urgent quadrant:
   tasks are done immediately and
   personally. This is called "Do
   First" quadrant and includes
   crises, deadlines, and problems.

The Eisenhower Matrix

2. Important/Not Urgent quadrant: tasks get an end date and
   then are done personally. This is called "Do Later" quadrant and
   includes management of relationships, planning, recreation, etc.
3. Unimportant/Urgent quadrant: most tasks should be delegated. It
   is called the "Delegate" quadrant, covering interruptions, certain
   meetings, and low-level activities.
4. Unimportant/Not Urgent quadrant: tasks are dropped. The quadrant
   is called "Eliminate" and includes time wasters.

We will learn more about the application of the Eisenhower Matrix to
time management in the next chapter.

While the time management tools of the first, second, and third-gen-
eration have made a significant contribution to helping people, many of us
are being turned off by them. Why is that? Because we feel chained to the
demands of a scheduler rather than that of the task at hand. As a result,

there is an emerging fourth generation of time-management concept that is different. It recognizes that time management is a misnomer; the challenge is not to manage time, but to manage ourselves. Rather than focusing on time and things, the fourth generation emphasizes essential activities such as enhancing relationships and accomplishing desired results.

The complexity of modern life and our apparent inabilities to control events raise some crucial questions: "what do we do about it?" or "is time management the real solution?" or "should people perhaps start simplifying their lives?" This material supports a new paradigm to solve this dilemma: move away from time management, which means managing schedules and task lists, to managing ourselves, which means focusing on what is important to us. This is the essence of personal management; this is the essence of Stepping Stone 4.

There is substantial scientific evidence that tremendous improvements in personal productivity can be achieved. Just listen to what British author and businessman Richard Koch (b.1950) once remarked: "There is never a shortage of time. In fact, we are positively awash with it. Unfortunately, we make good use of only 20 percent of our time."[74] During his research, Koch found out, for instance, that 20 percent of products of a business account for about 80 percent of sales. Applying the same 80-20 principle to personal activity, he confidently stated that: "20 percent of our time produces 80 percent of the results." This finding gives us tremendous potential for productivity improvement!

The shift from time management to self-management is a revolutionary concept. It requires a thorough understanding of its underlying principles, a continuous and conscious effort to internalize it, and a rigorous discipline in its application. But once mastered, this paradigm will liberate you from the oppression of the clock and will certainly provide you with the most modern management tool to accomplish your goals.

> REMEMBER: SHIFTING YOUR PARADIGM
> FROM "TIME MANAGEMENT" TO "PERSONAL
> MANAGEMENT" WILL INCREASE YOUR
> EFFECTIVENESS TREMENDOUSLY!

Moments of Reflection

1. What's your favorite definition of time?
2. Do you think you're always behind in what you're doing?
3. How do you currently cope with all daily activities? Do you feel overwhelmed?
4. Do you currently use any time management tool?
5. What is the Eisenhower Matrix?
6. What does the 80-20 rule say when applied to personal management?
7. What is the paradigm shift supported by Stepping Stone 4?

CHAPTER 14
THE MAGIC QUADRANT

—◆·◆·●·◆·◆—

"But seek ye first the kingdom of God, and his righteousness;
and all these things shall be added unto you." (Matthew 6:33)

L et me start with a well-known story worth repeating[75]:
    One evening, a father stood before his children with some items
on the table in front of him. The father said, "Watch what I'm doing and
learn from it."

He then wordlessly picked up a large empty jar and proceeded to fill it
with rocks about two inches in diameter. He then asked the children if the
jar was full. They agreed that it was full.

Then, he picked up some pebbles and poured them into the jar. He
shook the jar lightly until all pebbles rolled between the rocks. He asked
the children again if the jar was full. They all cried, "yes, it is fuller than
before." Next, the father picked up a fistful of sand and poured it into the
jar. The sand filled the remaining open areas of the pot. He asked: "Can I
add more stuff?" To which all kids cried, "No!"

"Now," said the father, "here is the lesson you have learned
this evening:

- The jar signifies your life
- The rocks are truly important things in life, such as family, health, and friends. If all else was lost, and only the rocks remained, your life would still be meaningful.
- The pebbles are other things which matter in your life, such as school, work, and recreation
- The sand signifies the remaining small stuff, for example, watching excessive TV or buying too many toys and unnecessary clothes."

The father continued: "if you put the sand into the jar first, there is no room for rocks or pebbles. The same is in life. If you spend all your time on the small stuff, you will never have room for the truly important things."

"Take care of the rocks first - things that really matter. Set your priorities right. The rest is just pebbles and sand."

In this chapter, we will explore together the concepts of important and urgent and see how we can create priorities based on these critical criteria. Then we will establish how the Eisenhower matrix introduced in the previous chapter can be transformed into the Four Quadrants tool to help us prioritize tasks. And finally, we will explore the power of the Magic Quadrant, which covers the activities that are of a long-term, preventive, educational, and relationship-building nature.

Urgent vs. Important

The key to understanding the core of the new paradigm of personal management is the ability to distinguish between what is urgent and what is important. For many people, if something is urgent, it must be relevant; and vice versa, if something is important, it must be immediate as well. Well, in quite a few cases, this is true, but actually, they define two fundamentally different types of situations or events. We will understand why in the next paragraphs, but first, we must explain these two critical terms:

Urgent[76] is that requiring immediate attention or response such as: answering the phone.

- The baby is crying in the other room.
- Fixing a broken car this afternoon so you can go to work tomorrow.
- Calling 911 when your house is on fire.

Urgent relates to time; it means now. You must act now, you cannot afford to wait. Synonyms to urgent are acute, pressing, dire, critical, immediate, compelling, and so on. They all convey a sense of immediacy, a feeling of running out of time. Related to the concept of urgent is the notion of urgency. Urgencies are those activities or situations that must be attended right away, such as putting out a fire or taking a child to the doctor. Urgencies are also called emergencies when an unforeseen combination of circumstances calls for immediate attention.

A few observations about urgencies as they relate to our daily activities:

- Since all urgencies require immediate attention, they interrupt the normal flow of the day and rob us of precious time.
- Some people call them surprises or crises because, in a sense, they harm our daily activities.
- Urgencies always come from outside; they cannot be created by our minds.

From a psychological viewpoint, an emergency puts the brain on high alert. A person affected by it not only recognizes the gravity of the situation but is experiencing an actual bodily response that makes it more likely that they will act. In an urgent case, the body releases chemicals that sharpen the mind, prepare the reflexes, and enable the body to react quickly.

Since most urgencies are unexpected, they are impossible to predict. We can only react to them when they arrive. However, to mitigate their impact, we should be prepared for them at all levels: physical, emotional, financial, etc. And it is here, where the wisdom and experience of an individual shows its strength.

Important[77] is an adjective meaning "marked by or indicative of significant worth or consequences." The related noun is importance, which is the quality or state of being important. Other words with similar or close meanings are significance, magnitude, consequence, or weight.

> REMEMBER: URGENT IS A SPRINT;
> IMPORTANT IS A MARATHON

In the context of Stepping Stone 4, important is that which relates, first of all, to your Christian faith. Your relationship with Christ is the foundation of your existence; it is the source of your life. Everything flows out from it, including your mission, roles, and goals. Therefore, it is of utmost importance. Once you understand that, all other significant things in life will follow, such as preservation of health, pursuing higher education, having a great family life, building good quality relations with friends, and so on.

Important things come mostly from within us, seldom from outside. Why is that? Because the mission, roles, and goals in life are our creation under the guidance to the Holy Spirit. They are not imposed on us from outside; they are born inside us by our free will. Important things generally do not have a short time span attached to them; they are not urgent. On the contrary, they take a long time to accomplish. Doing important things is like a marathon race. It requires planning, sustained training, a tough mental attitude, and excellent physical shape.

Since important affairs usually are not urgent, they must compete for your time. They are always at risk of being pushed aside by urgencies. So, it must be your choice to attend to them in a proactive, disciplined, and systematic manner. For if you do not do them, they remain undone. Therefore, essential things demand more initiative, more proactivity, more willpower. We must act with persistence to make them happen. Nothing forces you to work on important matters with deadlines way in the future, except your integrity of character, your will power, and personal discipline. This is the essence of personal management; this is the core of the knowledge found on the fourth Stepping Stone platform. Once practiced and internalized, this knowledge and way of acting become a powerful habit that will keep you going for the rest of your life. Nothing will stop you from accomplishing your goals—neither outside circumstances nor own weaknesses or moods. This is the incredible power of self-discipline!

Four Quadrants

Remember the Eisenhower Matrix from the previous chapter? It is the forerunner to The Four Quadrants of Time in the diagram below.[78] The diagram helps us visualize the interplay between urgency and importance, and how it reflects in our daily activities.

The Four Quadrants of Time

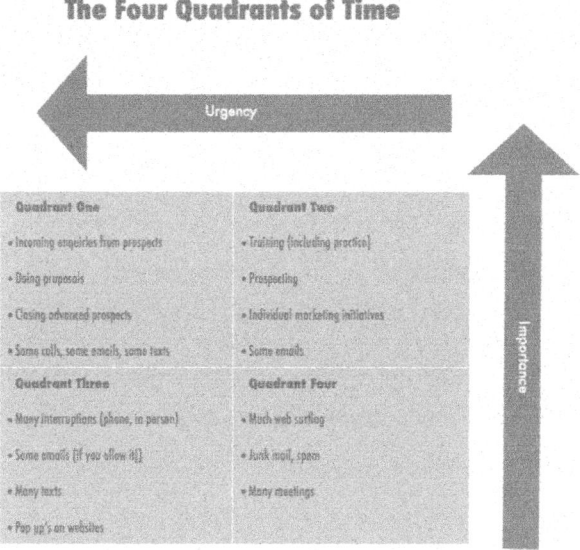

Quadrant One is both Urgent and Important. It deals with important activities that require immediate attention: finishing the proposal for tomorrow's meeting, fixing the car this afternoon so you can go to work in the morning, taking a late-evening phone call from the pastor at your church. We usually call the activities in Quadrant I, pressing issues, problems, or crises.

An excellent biblical example of acting on a problem that is both urgent and important was Moses climbing the mountain to talk to God. The Hebrew people were departing from the ways of the Lord, and it was necessary to straighten them out. It was of high urgency, too, because the Lord called on Moses to come to Him.

"God said to Moses, 'Climb higher up the mountain and wait there for me; I'll give you tablets of stone, the teachings and commandments that I've written to instruct them.'" (Exodus 24:12-13.)

We all face urgent/important activities in our daily lives and must learn to deal with them. Unfortunately, our behavior creates a crisis when we delay doing things on time and leave them to the last minute. In a typical dry humor, Mark Twain liked to say, *"Never put off till tomorrow what may be done day after tomorrow just as well,"* just to highlight the foolishness of procrastination. Working in the first Quadrant consumes many people, it stresses them out, and it exhausts them. When people spend most of their life in Quadrant I, they are beaten up by problems all day, every day, day after day. Such people live their lives in a constant crisis mode. Results are not hard to predict: stress, burnout, disillusionment, and a general sense of victimization. Let's nickname them Fire Fighters because they fight fires all day long and, as a result, cannot attend to their essential issues.

Quadrant Two is not urgent but important. Activities in this quadrant must be done consistently over a long time. They are like small drops of water filling a bucket overnight. Quadrant II is the quadrant of planning and prevention and is the key to effective personal and business management. Why is that? Because it prioritizes activities in order of their importance to the person's mission and goals, such as:

- Staying in constant touch with the Lord.
- Daily study for the end-of-term exam.
- Taking the car to service regularly, so it doesn't break down on you.
- Spending quality time with your spouse regularly.
- Taking time to build valuable relationships.
- Training your emergency response team before an emergency arises.
- Doing sports and planning R & R (relaxation and recreation) activities often to preserve your health and clear your mind.

But what is a priority? It is "something given or meriting attention before competing alternatives."[79] Setting priorities is the conscious process deciding which essential things must be done first. It is our capacity for personal management that sets the priorities correctly. Nobody else can do it for us. Setting priorities is, therefore, one of the most consequential activities of proactive people.

Prevention is one of the central activities belonging to Quadrant II. We all know the saying "an ounce of prevention is worth a pound of cure." Many organizations, by their own nature, must do preventive work before a crisis emerges, such as the military, police, or medical teams. So are all industries in modern times, which must plan today for what will happen next year. Teaching, training, and planning are also activities that belong to Quadrant II. All proactive people operate in Quadrant II because here they obtain maximum effectiveness, and a sense of control, satisfaction, balance, and predictability.

> **Blessed be the LORD my strength,**
> **which teacheth my hands to war,**
> **and my fingers to fight.**
> **Psalms 144:1**

Quadrant Three is urgent and not important. Many people spend a great deal of time in Quadrant III reacting to urgent things, assuming they are also important. But the reality is that the urgency of these matters is based on the priorities and expectations of others, not on their own preferences.

A typical inhabitant of Quadrant III is a gentle, polite person who always gives in to others' requests at the expense of her interests. "Please come with me to movies tonight," or, "Can you drive my kids to soccer this afternoon?" are legitimate requests that friends or relatives may ask of you. These pleas should be considered carefully before accepting them. For if they are interfering with your work on important issues, or they are excessive or abusive, they must be denied in a polite yet firm way. Persons living in Quadrant III are called, People Pleasers, Yes Men, or Yes Ladies. They excessively say yes most of the time to things relevant to other people, thus saying no to their important interests. They are too eager to please other people at their own expense.

Quadrant Four is not urgent and not important. People who operate in this quadrant watch too much TV, play games excessively, chat long hours over the phone, waste too much time hanging around with others. They have a short-term focus, feel victimized, and out of control. Typically, they experience shallow or broken relationships. In a sense, they live foolish lives. The results? Lack of capacity to move ahead, getting fired from jobs, and depending on others or government institutions for necessities. They feel worthless, guilty, and flaky.

REMEMBER: FOUR QUADRANT MATRIX IS A
GREAT TOOL FOR ESTABLISHING PRIORITIES

The Magic Quadrant

Quadrant II, the Magic Quadrant, is the core of effective personal management. It deals with elements that are not urgent but are essential. It deals with building relationships, long-range planning, staying in contact with the Lord, physical exercising, preventive maintenance. These are those things we know we need to do, but somehow seldom get around to doing, because they are not urgent.

Proactive people are opportunity-minded; they are not problem-minded. They feed opportunities and starve the problems; they think preventively. Of course, they have their share of Quadrant I crises, which require their immediate attention, but the number of their disasters is comparatively small because of prevention. And how do they do prevention? As soon as they solve a problem, proactive people perform a rigorous root cause analysis of it. They ask questions like: "What caused it? Was the crisis inherent to our process, or was it random? Which convergence of circumstances created it?" And finally, "What should we do to prevent its re-occurrence in the future?"

Studying carefully all tasks placed in the matrix should allow us to develop the most effective strategy for running our affairs. It must be focused on the following principles:

1. Operate most of the time in Quadrant II.
2. Shrink down Quadrant I as much as possible through prevention.
3. Stay out of Quadrants III by delegating.
4. Eliminate Quadrant IV completely.

Whether you are a student, a church leader, a homemaker, a computer programmer, or owner of a company, when you place your focus on Quadrant II activities, your effectiveness will increase dramatically. Your crises and problems will shrink to manageable proportions because you are now thinking ahead, analyzing the root causes of the problems, and doing the preventive things that keep situations from developing into crises in the first place.

One of the principles of working effectively in Quadrant II is establishing priorities and balancing their execution in a smart way. A few paragraphs earlier, we learned that priority is an important activity that you decide to do ahead of other essential activities. From a time perspective, we can say, therefore, that a priority has a sense of urgency. This begs the question: "is a priority the same as an urgency?" Not at all! A priority is your determination, your judgment, your call. It is your choice, it comes from within you, and it is a result of a conscious decision-making act. In contrast, an urgency comes from outside; it gets imposed on you. Balancing priorities is the process of harmoniously organizing and executing the top daily activities you need to do. You may have to adjust priorities in each role you play, such as being a father, spouse, friend, mentor, or business owner.

The objective of Quadrant II, the quadrant of self-management, is to effectively manage your daily activities from a center of solid principles. This center consists of knowing your mission, focusing on meaningful as well as the urgent, and the ability to use your willpower. The magic of the Quadrant II paradigm is that it empowers you to see activities through the lenses of importance rather than urgency. As you work to develop the Quadrant II paradigm, you will increase your ability to plan and execute every week of your life around your critical priorities.

> REMEMBER: THE MAGIC QUADRANT PROVIDES
> THE MAXIMUM PERSONAL EFFECTIVENESS

Moments of Reflection

1. Define urgency. Give instances of urgent things from last week.
2. Define importance. Provide examples of the essential activities you did lately.
3. What does the Four Quadrants of Time diagram tell you?
4. List activities from Quadrants I, II, III, and IV that you encountered yesterday.
5. What are the magic powers of Quadrant II? Why?
6. What are priorities? Provide examples of how you balance priorities daily.

CHAPTER 15
PERSONAL MANAGEMENT

————◆·◆·◆————

" Teaching us that, denying ungodliness and
worldly lusts, we should live soberly, righteously,
and godly, in this present world;" (Titus 2:12)

L et me start with a story[80]:
"How can you manage your time better?" a student asked Socrates
at one of his classes. To which the teacher replied:

*"It is true we all feel that time passes too fast during day, and we do
not have enough of it. That is why this question arises in your mind naturally. So, my observation of people shows me this: a hardworking person
has no problem with managing his time, he has enough of it. As a result, he
produces more. But a lazy one always has less time, he is always behind, and
he produces less. Remember: We all are having enough time. We simply do
not know how to use it properly."*

In this chapter, we will discuss in-depth what it means to move most
of your daily tasks in Quadrant II, the quadrant of long-term planning
and prevention. To do so, you must learn how to say No to trivial activities

and people that rob your precious time. And finally, we'll learn about the principles of self-management, specifically prioritizing, weekly planning, and daily execution.

Moving into Quadrant II

We learned in the previous chapter that the Magic Quadrant II covers activities that are important but not urgent such as long-term planning, relationship building, and prevention. Proactive people use it because it affords the maximum effectiveness. But what does it mean to move into Quadrant II? For someone who tries this paradigm for the first time, what should he do? How does he create more hours in the day to allow him to spend more time in this quadrant? Obviously, he cannot create more hours in the day, but, for sure, he can make better use of those available to him.

In the beginning, the only place to get more time for Quadrant II activities is to rob it from Quadrants III and IV. These are useless quadrants anyway, so robbing hours from them should not bother you at all. Regarding Quadrant I, since you cannot ignore the urgent and vital nature of its problems, you must pay attention to them as they come along. However, as the size of Quadrant I shrinks due to preventive actions taken in Quadrant II, more hours from it will become available to you. Your ultimate goal is to spend most of your time in the prevention quadrant, and only as needed in the firefighting quadrant. How do you take hours away from Quadrants III and IV? By saying a polite but firm no whenever activities arising from them knocking at your door. This means:

- Delegating tasks to other people.
- Screening incoming phone calls.
- Filtering emails, messages, and other social media communication channels.
- Skipping insignificant meetings.

- Limiting the length of personal and social chats.

In this way, over time, you should be able to shrink almost to zero the traditional time wasters that used to take much of your precious time in the past.[81]

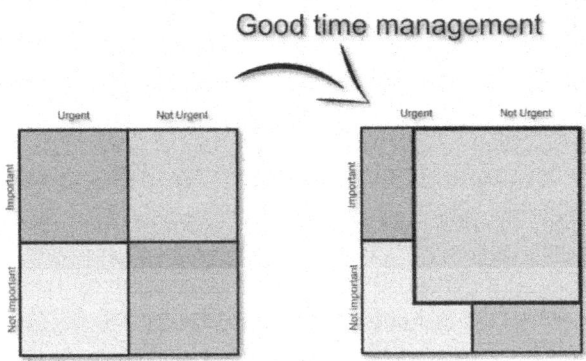

Good time management

After you become good at it, you will notice that the Magic Quadrant increases in size, while the other three decrease. Your goal is to shrink Quadrants III and IV to an insignificant size. Regarding unexpected crises that will still show up once in a while, you aim to solve them quickly and then spend the necessary time analyzing their root causes. The obvious beneficiary of this strategy is Quadrant II, the Prevention quadrant, where you now spend most of your time. This is a great pattern to follow; this is proper personal management!

Scheduling Tools

As you learn to work more and more in Quadrant II, you will need to use the organizing and scheduling tools of the fourth generation to maximize your effectiveness. You will find that most of them are either software apps or classic weekly planners. To be useful, they must meet several vital criteria.[82]

Consistency: Consistency assure there is harmony, unity, and integrity between your vision and mission, your roles and goals, your priorities, and plans. In the planner, there must be a place for your Personal Mission Statement, so you can always refer to it and adapt it if necessary. It also needs to be a place for the roles you play in life, and both long-term goals and short-term objectives.

Balance: Your tool should help keep your life in balance by clearly identifying your various roles and saving them right there in front of you.

Focus: You need a planner that allows easy changing and keeps you focused on prevention rather than handling crises. The best way to do this is to organize your time every week. You can still adapt and prioritize daily, but the fundamental thrust should be controlling the week.

A people-orientation: While you can think in terms of efficiency in dealing with time, a principle-centered person thinks in terms of effectiveness in dealing with people. There are times when living in Quadrant II requires the subordination of schedules to people.

Flexibility: Your planning tool must be your servant, never your master. Since it has to work for you, it should be tailored to your style, needs, and particular ways.

Portability: Your tools should also be portable to allow you to carry it with you all the time.

In the current age, the best planning tools are software apps that run on multiple devices fully integrated and wholly synced with one another. For instance, you use a laptop at work and a smartphone or tablet at home or when traveling. From either device, you should be able to check or modify your schedule, and modifications should instantly show up on all of them. This will give you tremendous flexibility and portability at all times and from all locations.

> REMEMBER: THE ONLY WAY TO OBTAIN HIGHER
> EFFECTIVENESS IS TO MOVE YOUR OPERATIONS IN
> THE MAGIC QUADRANT

Saying No

We just learned that moving more work into Quadrant II requires us to say No to specific activities or people.[83] Doing this is a matter of personal discipline but also having people skills.

<u>Saying No to Others</u>

Many people are not comfortable refusing other people, particularly friends, relatives, neighbors, or business associates. Saying No is inherently hard because you do not want to offend or make unhappy the other person. Yet it can be done elegantly as described below. Suppose you are face -to- face with your good friend, who's asking you to do something you do not want to do. Look her straight in the eyes, smile, and say a soft no surrounded by two affirmative phrases as follows:

1. Open with a positive sentence using a friendly voice.
2. Say No using a softer tone.
3. Close with something positive using an enthusiastic voice.

Let's say she's inviting you to a party over the weekend. However, you cannot attend because you have to study for an exam next week. Your refusal should sound like this:

"Deborah, you know I love your parties very much; they are so much fun" (opening statement in a friendly voice).

"Unfortunately, this time, I cannot come" (softer voice).

"But I promise you something: I'll take you to the movies next week" (enthusiastic voice).

As you can see, no justification is needed unless you feel it's necessary to offer it, or your interlocutor asks for one. If this is the case, your explanation must be truthful: *"Debbie, I have this darn exam on Monday, which is so important to me. I simply have to pass it with a high mark, so I need to study every minute I have available."*

> **But above all things...**
> **let your yea be yea;**
> **and your nay, nay;**
> **lest ye fall into condemnation.**
> **James 5:12**

Saying No to Your Weaknesses

Saying no to yourself means overcoming your weaknesses and moods when it comes to daily choices. The object of our decision may be a routine daily activity or a thing having no particular significance. Saying no, however, is essential because of its training value. If you learn to say no repeatedly to your weaknesses and moods, it becomes a healthy habit that will serve you well in the future.

But let's face it: refusing yourself is a difficult thing to do, particularly when you're still in training. But it can be learned and internalized through practice. Indeed, it is a slow training process with ups and downs but with extraordinary rewards in the end. The key to success is to start small, to be demanding on yourself, and watch your progress from one week to another. This will increase your self-esteem and integrity of character. You are now right to your own word, precisely when nobody watches you. This is supreme character integrity!

Saying No to Temptation

Much more difficult is saying no to temptations[84] which are enticements to sin of a higher order. Temptations are much harder to reject than overcoming personal moods because they come straight from Satan, the master tempter. He constantly prowls the earth, looking to drive a wedge between God and His children. Unfortunately, for many Christians, evil temptations are part of their daily lives. The importance of avoiding and overcoming temptations is underlined by its inclusion in the Lord's prayer.

On the path to spiritual maturity, every temptation should become a step forward rather than a stumbling block. Why is that? Because it is as much an occasion to do the right thing as it is to do the wrong one. Temptation simply provides the choice, but it is up to you what to choose. Many believers are frightened and demoralized by tempting thoughts, feeling guilty that they aren't beyond temptation. They feel ashamed just for being tempted. But what they forget is that being tempting is not a sin. Temptation becomes sin only when you give in to it. Jesus was tempted, yet he never sinned. We can look at temptations as opportunities for us to show God that we can overcome them. Every temptation is an occasion to prove your character and your faith.

REMEMBER: WE'RE ALL VULNERABLE TO
TEMPTATION, THEREFORE ALWAYS BE VIGILANT

Here is a time-tested practical defensive strategy against temptation:
- Clad yourself in the armor of God all the time, as instructed in Ephesians 6:10-17.

- Stay alert and be on guard. Even when you feel safe from the Evildoer, stay vigilant. We must never let down our guard and think we're beyond temptation.
- Anticipate and prevent it. Common sense tells you that if you want to avoid a street fight, don't go on that street. God warns us never to get cocky and overconfident but always to stay humble. Remember that our flesh is weak, and given the right circumstances, most of us are capable of any sin.

Becoming a Magic Quadrant Manager

Here are some tips on becoming a successful Magic Quadrant manager.[85] They include practical issues such as prioritizing, planning, and execution, as well as dealing with your comfort zone, overcoming fear, and finding courage.

Principles of Self-Management

The following are three principles required for successful self-management in Quadrant II.

Prioritize: This means to put first things first, to prioritize all your essential activities. Always allocate blocks of time for your marathon activities, such as studying, building relationships, prevention, etc. Crises, when they come, should get top ranking in terms of attention, time, and resources. Always include the root-cause analysis of the problem that caused the crisis in the first place.

Plan weekly; execute daily: Your important things must always show in your planner as blocks of time allocated on a daily or weekly basis. Do not forget that your essential things take place in all roles of your life. For instance, block out time for meetings with your associates, working at your desk, visiting a client, attending the PTA meeting at night, or taking the family to the movies. Once you have prioritized your day, schedule the other smaller things around those priorities.

Act, review, and act again: Success in self-management happens only if you are relentless in what you do. In other words, stay on a priority until it's solved, even if it takes several iterations to achieve the desired outcome. And remember, the quality of work is more important than the schedule. If getting the job done properly takes a little longer than initially thought, so be it!

> REMEMBER: A MISSED DEADLINE IS
> EASILY FORGOTTEN, BUT A POOR QUALITY
> OUTCOME IS NEVER FORGIVEN!

Comfort, Fear, and Courage

As a self-manager in training in Quadrant II, you will soon find out that acting on new principles is not that easy. Planning and executing in the preventive quadrant require courage, and often you will be stretched out of your comfort zone. Let's provide some details.[86]

The comfort zone represents things, activities, and people with which you are already familiar. They typically include your car, drinking your morning coffee in a leisurely way, your church, your family, and friends. Another way to look at the comfort zone is as a place or situation where one feels safe, at ease, and without stress. The comfort zone will never test your abilities and determination. For instance, the phrase 'rock climbing pushes many people beyond their comfort zones' indicates an activity that clearly is out of one's comfort zone. Therefore, the question becomes, 'what keeps people from moving out of their comfort zone?' It is the fear of the unknown.

Fear is a horrible emotion caused by the threat of danger, pain or harm, real or imaginary, or even ordinary yet unknown circumstances. Fear is such a powerful emotion that it can easily override all other feelings, logic, or priorities. Fear is one of the strongest motivators of human behavior: fear of death, fear of the enemy, fear of your boss, fear of losing your job, and so on. But fear may also be present when smaller things need to happen, such as speaking in public, meeting new people, moving to a new school, or defending your values. In essence, fear is an illusion nonexistent in the physical world — it is neither tangible nor visible. But it lives in our minds and manifests itself through our actions. Unfortunately, we bring fear to life quickly, many times without need. So, the question becomes, 'How do you overcome fear?' And the answer is, 'with courage.'

Courage is the capacity to act toward a worthwhile goal despite the presence of risk, uncertainty, and fear. It takes courage for soldiers to advance in the face of enemy fire; it takes courage for an employee to stand up to an abusive boss; it takes courage for a boy to face his bullying peers; it takes courage for someone to do new things; it takes courage for a young manager to move her activities into Quadrant II.

"Be strong and of a good courage; be not afraid, neither be thou dismayed: for the LORD thy God *is* with thee whithersoever thou goest." (Joshua 1:9)

The courage zone represents everything else that is not into your comfort zone. The courage zone makes us uncomfortable because of its uncertainties, such as changes, pressures, and the risk of failure. It will most certainly test our courage, abilities, and determination to go through it. Nearly all people live their lives in their comfort zone, and only occasionally will venture out of it. But living just in the comfort zone brings stagnation, boredom, and limitations. The courage zone is the one that makes us grow, tests our limits, and fulfill our potential. It is only here where we discover who we truly are, and where we can conquer ourselves. Sir Edmund Hillary, the man who first climbed Mount Everest, the highest peak on Earth, said, *"it was not the mountain I conquered, but myself."* And Sir Winston Churchill reminded us that *"All great deeds are done in the face of great fear."*

Delegation

Becoming a successful manager requires learning how to delegate. Remember that in the Eisenhower Matrix, the third quadrant is called delegate. Delegation is the simplest method of freeing your valuable time from daily chores that can be done by people less qualified. Webster's definition of delegation[87] is "the act of empowering to act for another." From a business perspective, it means "giving responsibility and authority to someone to complete a clearly defined and agreed upon task while you retain ultimate responsibility for its success."

Delegations are of two kinds: do delegation and stewardship delegation.[88]

Do delegation means, 'do this, do that, and tell me when it's done.' Most supervisors employ this type of delegation. They use team members to do urgent, routine, or fragmented tasks, telling them in detail how to do them. They focus on methods, rather than on results. It is the traditional delegating paradigm, which, unfortunately, is not very effective.

Stewardship delegation, also known as authority delegation, is based on a paradigm of appreciation of capacities, the imagination, the conscience, and the free will of other team members. It gives people a choice of methods and makes them responsible for results. It indeed takes more training time in the beginning, but it's time well invested. Stewardship delegation brings maximum effectiveness to the team, freeing more time for the supervisors, and empowering the subordinates. It is the best way to delegate!

REMEMBER: STEWARDSHIP DELEGATION IS A TOOL
THAT ALL MANAGERS MUST LEARN AND USE

An excellent scriptural exemplification of stewardship is how Jesus delegated authority to his disciples: "And he said unto them, Go ye into all the world, and preach the gospel to every creature." (Mark 16:15)

In our temporal world, stewardship delegation involves clear communications, upfront mutual understanding, and commitment regarding expectations in five areas:

1. **Results:** Work out a clear understanding of what needs to be completed, focusing on results, not on methods. Have the person understand and commit to them in terms of quality and timeline.

2. **Guiding principles:** Offer general guidelines and identify the parameters within which the person should operate. Provide considerable authority for decision-making, as long as it is applied within the guidelines. Based on prior experience, point out the potential failure paths, what not to do. Keep the responsibility for the results with the person--to do whatever it takes within the guidelines.

3. **Resources:** Identify the human, financial, technical, or organizational resources the person can draw on to accomplish his mission.

4. **Responsibilities**: Set up standards of performance to assess the results and the specific timeframe for reporting and evaluation.

5. **Consequences**: Specify what will happen, both good and bad, as a result of the final evaluation. This could include such things as verbal or financial rewards, different job assignments (up or down), and other natural consequences tied into the overall mission of the organization.

Let's now move on to the next chapter titled *You are Disciplined*, which is the concluding chapter in Stepping Stone 4.

Moments of Reflection

1. Describe what it means to move your operations to Quadrant II.
2. What planner/organizer do you currently use? Is it suitable for the new paradigm of operating in the prevention quadrant?
3. How do you say No to others? And to yourself?
4. Which are the principles of self-management?
5. What does it take to get out of your comfort zone?
6. Give examples of things you usually do in your comfort zone.
7. Give examples of past things you did in the courage zone.
8. What is do delegation? What are its shortcomings?
9. What is stewardship delegation? Can you apply it to the family? Or at work?

CHAPTER 16
YOU ARE DISCIPLINED

———•◆•———

"Whoso loveth instruction loveth knowledge: but he
that hateth reproof *is* brutish." (Proverbs 12:1)

tephen Hawking, a name that resonates with the power of the mind,
the victory of intellect over adversity, died at 76 on March 15, 2018.
Following are a few excerpts from an article published in Times of India
on that day.[89]

" Now, what made the ailing man a genius of mind and a 'cult figure'?
Was it his willpower or his physical affliction that strengthened his mind?
He was diagnosed with a crippling disease at the age of 21, but in respect
of his genius, fortune favored him since then. His scientific work got richer
and better, and he quickly set a succession of scientific insights on his theory
of black holes. The man, whose body was so frail and seemed to fail his
genius, did not give up. It would not be wrong to say that technology saved
him. In fact, this was only the beginning of what led him to become the
greatest scientist of the age.

Some experts say that perhaps Hawking was wrongly diagnosed, and
this is the reason for his surviving over half a century. Also, doctors say that

in the case of Hawking, the disease spread slower than it does in most of the patients, giving him way more time than the others. Hawking himself said, "I have been lucky that my condition has progressed more slowly than is often the case. But it shows that one need not lose hope."

In this final chapter of Stepping Stone 4, we will learn about free will, willpower, and how to train them. We will also make a summary of the teachings of Stepping Stone 4, *I am Disciplined*.

The Power of Willpower

Free Will

Let us examine first what free will is. Free will is a difficult philosophical and theological concept about which exists a vast body of literature.[90] From a Scriptural perspective, free will is the gift received through the grace of God, to let us humans make our choices. From a secular perspective, free will can be defined in several ways: (a) the ability to choose between different possible courses of action unimpeded, (b) the power of acting without the constraints of necessity, (c) the ability to operate at one's discretion. Free will is closely linked to the notions of responsibility, praise, guilt, sin, and other judgments that apply only to actions that are freely chosen. Free will is, therefore, the ability to make conscious choices. We all have free will and make our own choices, even if these are to obey the commands of others.

Free will relates to want and desire. If you do not want something very much, then the will to succeed is likely to be weak. On the other hand, if you have a strong desire, then you'll be more likely to succeed. Why is that? Because your much stronger free will shall, in turn, create persistence, which eventually leads to success. Remember the old proverb: "Where there is a will, there is a way."

Willpower

There are many common names for willpower: determination, drive, resolve, self-discipline, self-control. However, psychologists characterize willpower in several more specific ways:[91]

- The ability to delay gratification, resisting short-term temptations to meet long-term goals.
- The capacity to override an unwanted thought, feeling, or impulse.
- The ability to employ a 'cool' cognitive system of behavior rather than a 'hot' emotional system.
- Conscious, effortful regulation of the self by the self.

The willpower can also be regarded as the motivation to exercise free will. A person with strong willpower will assert decisions even in front of adverse circumstances or strong opposition. In contrast, a person with weak willpower will give in easily.

The power of our willpower is genuinely amazing. It can transform each of us into a well-designed machine that moves tirelessly, with precision, consistency, and high efficiency to accomplish the goals that we set out to do. The performance of this machine does not depend on the circumstances around it or our moods and emotions. It will continue to work until we tell it to stop. The willpower can also be called, in an amusing way, 'the boss inside me' because it always yells orders from inside to me on the outside.

Self-Discipline

Regarding self-discipline, we can safely say that it is the external display of the willpower.[92] Much commitment, effort, and energy are required to develop and use self-discipline. Why is that? To understand this better, it is useful to draw a parallel with an essential law of physics that deals with energy, the law of entropy.[93]The law of entropy states that everything in the universe eventually moves from order to disorder, and entropy is the measurement of that change. An orderly system requires energy to stay that way; if energy is no longer applied, the system falls slowly into a state of disorder.

> With self-discipline
> most anything is possible.
> Theodore Roosevelt

It is the same in our personal life. For instance, if you want to keep your room neat, you have to spend energy every day to pick up stuff and put it in its proper place; otherwise, in a couple of days, the room will become messy. Applying the concept of entropy to human society, it would result that our lives would slip towards a state of disorder if we do not actively put in the effort and energy to keep them in order. Just think of the well-known saying "keeping your ducks in a row." Can it be done without expending relentless effort? Of course, not! So, if you want to be disciplined and keep your life in line, you must use much effort and energy to achieve it.

The proper use and application of willpower is a hallmark of proactive people. No athlete, manager, scientist, doctor, performing artist, military personnel, or schoolteacher can achieve much without having inside them a high dose of willpower revealed through self-discipline. They all must train long years, work endless hours each day, and make personal sacrifices to become what they want to be. It has been so for centuries, it is true nowadays, and it will be so well into the future.

> REMEMBER: WILLPOWER AND SELF-
> DISCIPLINE ARE THE COMMON
> DENOMINATORS OF GREAT ACHIEVERS

Willpower Training

Willpower and self-discipline are not gifted at birth. They cannot be inherited from parents; they must be acquired. That's why an orderly atmosphere at home, a disciplined classroom at school, and a strong-willed football coach are important factors in the early development of a young mind and body. Unfortunately, these days, the concepts of discipline and willpower are no longer taught to students at school or at home as in the old days. As a result, many children nowadays grow up to become undisciplined young adults lacking willpower.

This trend in a young person's life must be stopped and reversed. So, the question becomes, 'How does a young adult acquire willpower and self-discipline?' There is only one answer: through systematic, well-thought-out, and extended training. Such training becomes a critical phase in developing your Christlike Diamond Soul character.

Training one's willpower and self-discipline is not an easy task. It is a long-term proposition that will test your commitment and determination. It will definitely take you out of your comfort zone into the rougher and more demanding courage zone. It will demand your toil, sweat, and blood but, in the end, it will reward you greatly.[94]

Training your willpower and self-discipline requires a progression that begins with little things and builds up slowly toward more demanding jobs. Here are a few sound rules and practices to follow on a daily basis:

1. **Create a neat new self:** Start with making a new self in terms of how you look and dress, even when you are alone. Always be neatly groomed and wear clean and decent clothing. Be proud when you look in the mirror and see your new self. Remember, when you're at home, you don't do this for others to see; do it for your benefit, to express the value you place on yourself. The clothes you select should express your personality and be appropriate for the occasion. Being appropriately dressed and looking your best is also important when

you place yourself in front of others. In situations when you need to be persuasive if you want people to listen to you, follow the rule 'dress the message.' The clothes you wear and how you look will change the way people hear what you say.

2. **Create order in your environment**: Start with keeping your room, house, office space, and car clean, functional, and pleasant. Get rid of clutter, junk, and useless things that distract your attention and confuse your mind. "A neat room is a sign of a neat mind" - this is what our parents used to tell us. Make your bed every morning, fold, and store your clothing after undressing, clean up the kitchen table after you eat. This is particularly important if you are a parent, since you are the role model, the kids will observe and follow in their behavior.

3. **Create an orderly daily schedule:** Your regular schedule should look the same every weekday. Wake up at the same time, preferably early in the morning. Include in your morning routine a brisk walk outdoors or some indoor exercising. This will get your body and mind ready and energized for the day. If you work from home, get to your desk at the same time every day. Take hourly breaks to stretch your legs and rest your eyes. Have healthy and nutritional meals every day at the same time. Have an evening routine that is relaxing and pleasant. Always reserve time for devotion. Go to bed at the same time; avoid working too late.

4. **Push your limits:** In whatever you do, try to push yourself harder and demand more of yourself. If you do pushups every morning, start with a few, then gradually add more. This will train not only your muscles but also your willpower. When the body hurts, push it a bit harder to find its limits.

5. **Get out of your Comfort Zone:** Moving out of your comfort zone requires courage, which in turn is activated by willpower. Whenever

you want to do new things that make you feel anxious, tell yourself, 'I will gather all my willpower to do this even if I have to die doing it' or, 'this thing cannot be stronger than me.' In the beginning, do things that are not that difficult, so you gain confidence in your ability to operate in the Courage Zone. Then slowly take on more difficult tasks, those requiring more courage and determination on your part. Your goal is to practice, master, and internalize these character traits until they become your most trusted habits.

A word of caution: willpower should never become fanatical, or self-discipline turns into an obsessive or unhealthy habit. They should just be useful tools at your disposal to achieve your noble goals in life. Use them with wisdom, flexibility, and respect for others!

> REMEMBER: WILLPOWER AND SELF-DISCIPLINE ARE CHARACTER TRAITS THAT MUST BE PRACTICED OVER AND OVER EVERY DAY

Standing on Stepping Stone 4: You Are Disciplined!

The Christian virtues of Temperance and Diligence are at the foundation of Stepping Stone 4. Since the word temperance is seldom used in current English, we're going to use synonyms such as self-control or self-restraint. Similarly, the meaning of diligence is better understood if we use words like persistent effort, hard work, tenacity, and so on. We should say, therefore, that the principles of self-control and hard work should form the base of Christian self-discipline. One of the critical elements in managing ourselves is understanding the concepts of time, urgency, and importance because they let us develop tools for prioritizing tasks. One such tool is the Eisenhower Matrix, which classifies jobs according to their importance and urgency. The Eisenhower Matrix tells us to focus our energies in the so-called Magic Quadrant, which contains tasks that are important but have no urgency attached to them. This kind of job relates to our mission, roles, and long-term goals. They will include staying close to God, developing healthy lifestyle habits, getting a better education, building relationships, planning, and prevention activities.

Stepping Stone 4 advocates the paradigm shift from time management to personal management to achieve higher effectiveness in dealing with ourselves and executing our daily tasks. Personal management uses the principles of prioritization, planning weekly but executing daily, and acting, reviewing, and acting again. It requires us to move out of our comfort zone and start working in the courage zone. For this, we require willpower and self-discipline. These are critical traits of a Diamond Soul character and can only be acquired and mastered through willful, long-term training.

"I am disciplined" is a considerable achievement of every Christian. Those who master it should be grateful to the Holy Spirit for his guidance and encouragement. When you tell yourself, "I am disciplined," you acknowledge your commitment to using willpower and self-discipline in life. Self-discipline will give you the tool to execute the tasks necessary to accomplish your goals regardless of external circumstances or your moods. By using and mastering it, you will become unstoppable. Way to go, Christian warrior!

This is how you should think and what you do as the owner of willpower and master of self-discipline:

- Understand the value of time, one of your most valuable assets.
- Understand the concepts of urgent and important; use them to prioritize tasks by employing the Eisenhower Matrix.

- Understand and value the critical importance of moving activities in the Magic Quadrant II. But you are also prepared to face unexpected urgencies, which show up in Quadrant I.
- Delegate activities of Quadrant III and say NO to triviality and time-wasters of Quadrant IV.
- Learn to say no to others in a polite yet firm way.
- Know that willpower and self-discipline are the only instruments you have to convert goals into accomplishments.
- Understand and use the principles of stewardship delegation.
- Prioritize and plan every week but execute daily.
- Train your self-discipline daily by creating a new self, keeping an orderly environment, and following a regular daily schedule.
- When making value judgments, you are using the principle, people and quality are more important than cost and time schedules.

Moments of Reflection

1. On a scale from 1 to 10, rate your current level of willpower.
2. What do you need to do to improve it?
3. Provide examples of a lack of self-discipline in your current daily schedule.
4. How will you train your willpower and self-discipline?
5. How often did you get out of your comfort zone last week?
6. What are the traits of a disciplined person?

POLISHING YOUR CHARACTER

—•◆•—

Virtues: Patience, Justice and Kindness

"For thou wilt light my candle: the LORD my God will
enlighten my darkness."
Psalms 18:28

CHAPTER 17
ADDING NEW FACETS TO
YOUR DIAMOND SOUL

---·◆·◆·◆·◆·---

"That the man of God may be perfect, thoroughly
furnished unto all good works."
(2 Timothy 3:17)

L et's take note of what Seth Horowitz of the New York Times says about
the skill of listening:[95]

*"Listening is a skill that we're in danger of losing in a world of digital
distraction and information overload."*

Similarly, the opinion of Valerie Brown:[96]

*"Listening, deeply listening, is a greatly underrated life and leadership
skill. Perhaps one reason for this is that our western culture often privileges
the fast-talking, think-on-your-feet mode of being. Listening for genuine
connection and understanding, listening that engenders trust and authen-
ticity, asks so much of us. I was reminded of this popular wisdom about listening: When two people are in dialogue, there are actually three conversations
going on. The first conversation is the external conversation between the two
people. The other two conversations are each person's internal dialogue."*

In this last stepping stone, we learn other cherished skills which will enable us to become even better fighters in Jesus Christ. Once such skills are acquired, practiced, and mastered, they will turn into new habits of effectiveness. At the same time, they become new facets of our Diamond Soul character. As discussed elsewhere in this material, adding new facets to a diamond involves two stages, cutting and polishing. Cutting requires great skills, but the process is not too long. In contrast, polishing the cuts will take a much longer time. In fact, this stage will last a lifetime. For this reason, we consider that Patience should be the noteworthy Christian virtue associated with this platform of learning. The other two virtues should be Justice and Kindness.

Stepping Stone 5 deals exclusively with the world around us. It instructs us in three crucial areas: (i) how to build meaningful relationships based on mutual interest, (ii) how to influence others through effective communications, and finally (iii) how to work creatively with other people.

Relationships Based on Trust and Mutual Interest

"Look not every man on his own things, but every man also on the things of others." (Philippians 2:4)

Relationships

Being in quality relationships is one of the greatest desires of the human soul. Most celebrated works of art, literature, poetry, and music are about bonds of love, friendship, loyalty, and sacrifice. The Bible is evident in how God views them: they all must be based on love. In fact, one can argue that the Holy Book is about how we, humans, relate with God and with one another. Love is, therefore, the essence of interpersonal human bonds.

Trust

Trust is the foundation of all human associations, from unplanned encounters to true friendships, and from family ties to affairs between nations.[97] It governs all interactions we have with each other. In essence, trust is believing that the person who is trusted will do what is expected. Recent studies have demonstrated that people have a natural disposition to trust and that this inclination results from the way the human brain is wired.

A practical way to think about relationships is to treat them as bank accounts. American author Steven Covey (1936-2012) calls them relationship bank accounts, or RBAs.[98] A relationship bank account is a metaphor for the emotional trust and confidence you have in a relationship. The RBA is like a checking account at the bank. At it, you make deposits to increase the balance and take withdrawals to reduce it. In like manner, in a relationship, you make deposits to improve it and take withdrawals to weaken it. A strong and healthy relationship is always the result of steady deposits made over long periods. Here are some examples of RBA deposits and withdrawals in human relationships.[99]

RBA DEPOSITS	RBA WITHDRAWALS
Keep promises.	Break promises.
Do small acts of kindness.	Be a jerk.
Try to understand.	Do not care or listen.
Be loyal.	Be deceitful.
Show integrity.	Be dishonest.
Set clear expectations.	Set confusing or unrealistic expectations.
Say you're sorry.	Be indifferent.
Forgive.	Be arrogant.

Mutual Interest

Mutual interest is the attitude of trust and willingness to cooperate with others in search of shared benefits. The love of people must be at its foundation. We can also call it the mindset of thinking win-win. Achieving it requires a paradigm shift from a state of mind of scarcity to one of abundance. This means being concerned not only about your own needs, but also about the needs of others at the same time. It advocates taking a proactive approach to human interactions, steering them toward achieving mutual benefits, and managing them proactively.

Abundance Mentality

To understand abundance, we must contrast it with the scarcity. Scarcity is defined as the state of being scarce or in short supply. It refers to the underlying economic problem in society, i.e., the gap between limited environmental resources and theoretically limitless human wants. Scarcity is the most popular outlook in life. *"I do not have enough money," "I do not have time," "I am not smart enough,"* and *"My house is too small"* are well-known phrases that come up often in daily conversations. A good number of people possess a scarcity mentality because they perceive life around them as offering limited opportunities, satisfactions, or rewards.

Abundance is the opposite of scarcity. Abundance means a large quantity of something, a state of plentifulness and prosperity. In a sense, abundance or poverty is the result of a judgment call about the existence of material possessions, intellectual abilities, and spiritual life. If you think plenty, you have a paradigm of affluence; if you feel scarcity, your model is one of poverty. This is easily observable by contrasting these two attitudes: *"I will share with you the little I have,"* which can be stated by a poor person.

Or, *"I can't share it with you because there isn't enough for me,"* which may be uttered by a wealthy individual.

**Look not every man
on his own things,
but every man also
on the things of others.
Philippians 2:4**

Abundance mentality is the proper paradigm for human relations: there is enough for you and me; there is enough for all of us. Its source is the infinite love of God. Abundance is the foundation for thinking positively and creatively about fulfilling the material, emotional, and spiritual needs of other people. Plenty is the source of two critical mindsets when dealing with people: give to others and demand from others. Abundance mentality leads to altruism and courage; scarcity mentality leads to egoism and fear. The source of scarcity outlook is the observation of what's outside us, i.e., the surrounding environment. In contrast, the source of abundance mentality is the contemplation of what's inside us, i.e., the fruits of the Holy Spirit and the content of our character.

The WIN-LOSE Matrix

A fitting way to understand human relations is to look at them through the prism of who wins and who loses in a relationship. If we arrange the words **win** and **lose** in a matrix, we will get four possible outcomes, as shown in the table below.[100]

win - lose	lose - win
lose - lose	win - win

These four outcomes can be regarded as four possible methods to manage human relations.

WIN - LOSE

The first method in managing human relations is by adopting the win-lose attitude. Win-lose is also known as the rat race. Win-lose is a paradigm towards life that says the pie of success is small, and if you get a larger piece, there is less for me. Win-lose is competitive, selfish, and full of arrogance. *"I must win; I must be first because I'm better than you."* This technique of managing relations is applied by people who consider themselves strong, competitive, and aggressive. It is based on a mindset of the comparison *"I am better than you; therefore, I must be above you"* and on one of competitiveness, *"I must win; therefore, you must lose."*

Examples of win-lose people are bullies, authoritative bosses, rude and inconsiderate persons, overbearing parents, etc. While it is true that being strong and competitive may be useful in specific fields such as sports, the military, businesses, etc., they are not valuable for human relations. Why is that? Because they do not lead to equality and happiness in relationships. The domineering person wants to force his view on you. They want quick wins at your expense.

LOSE - WIN

The Lose-Win method is the opposite of win-lose. It is the attitude of people who mistakenly consider themselves negotiators or soothers. They want to be perceived as nice guys. Unfortunately, trying to please others all the time doesn't work. It just shows how frail you actually are. Lose-win looks respectful on the surface, but it is as dangerous and unproductive. Lose-win denotes lacking strength, not kindness. It is easy to give in, all in the name of being a soother.

Why is lose-win unhealthy? Simply because you'll find yourself setting lower and lower expectations for yourself and compromising your standards forever. Giving in to peer pressure is lose-win. Perhaps you don't want to go to the ballgame, but the group insists you come. So, you give in just to show you're a team player. What happens? You lose, and they win, of course. As a result, you don't feel good about yourself. Adopting lose-win as your attitude toward life is a mistake. People will always take advantage of you and for sure will start abusing you.

LOSE - LOSE

This is method number three. Lose-Lose is the most destructive attitude of all. It is created by hatred and stupidity. It is used by people whose life centers are their enemies or when someone becomes obsessed with the other person. Such people are prepared to go down the drain as long as their enemy goes down with them. Lose-lose is employed in hopeless situations or when reasoning is blinded by anger and revenge. For instance, lose-lose happens when two win-lose people get together and say to each other: *"If you want to win at any cost, and I want to win at any cost, let's fight it out."* And they do, and in most cases, they both end up losing.

WIN-WIN

This is the fourth method. Win-Win is a conviction that everyone can win. Win-win is based on an abundance mentality; it is founded on the belief that there is plenty of success to go around. Win-win is both attractive and hard at the same time. The parties tell each other: "I won't intimidate you, but I won't be your pushover, either." When thinking win-win, you care about other people and want them to succeed. However, you also care about yourself, and want to achieve as well.

The wonder of thinking win-win is that it always creates more. It opens up the door for unlimited creativity and fruitful cooperation to the benefit of all parties. Moreover, it not only produces more results, but it also fills your heart with satisfaction. So, the relationship becomes highly effective.

The secret to thinking win-win is found in your character. It all begins with you. If you are insecure deep inside and have not paid the price in effort, sweat, and tears to win the Diamond Soul character, it will be impossible to think win-win. You will feel threatened by other people. It will be hard to be happy for their successes or to share recognition. Only strong, independent people can think of sharing the win with others. Personal security, found in Diamond Soul character, is the foundation for thinking win-win.

The other requirement to successfully adopting a win-win mindset is to eliminate the words competition and comparison from your vocabulary. If you want to build a mutually beneficial and pleasant relationship with someone, you cannot compete or compare yourself with the other party. Compete with yourself to get better month after month - yes. Compete in sports - yes. But competing with each other in a precious relationship is not healthy. The same holds for the act of comparing. Yes, examine how you grow from one year to another. But no, do not compare yourself with your spouse or try to outdo her. Statements like *"Honey, how come you cannot bring home as much money as I do?"* or *"Don't you see I work twice as much as you do?"* are not respectful at all and will never lead to thinking win-win.

NOTHING

Besides the four attitudes resulting from the win-win matrix, there is another one that must be mentioned. It is the fifth approach, called nothing. It is used in relationships that either are ending or cannot get off the ground. For instance, a marriage ending up in divorce indicates the parties have decided to select nothing instead of trying to fix the marriage. This method can also be adopted before a potential relationship begins in earnest. Take a couple who decides to split after some time spent together. Why do they do it? Probably both of them have figured out they cannot have a win-win marriage, so they elect to stop it right there.

MUTUAL ADVANTAGE OR NOTHING

This is the new paradigm emerging from the win-win attitude: mutual advantage or nothing. Mutual advantage means that we both get equal benefits at the practical level, as well as a healthy, pleasant relationship at the emotional level. Nothing means that if we cannot find an overall win-win solution for the contemplated relationship, we will not get involved in it.

Win-Win is the attitude that demands us to search tirelessly for mutual benefits in human relations. Not only that, but also to put constant effort in maintaining the win-win character of the relationship. The sad truth is that even if we start on a win-win footing, if we're not careful enough, the relationship may degenerate quickly into something else. How can this be? Well, because either people and circumstances change, or someone finds a loophole in the agreement and tries to take advantage of it. In other words, they try to convert the existing win-win into a win-lose relationship. That is why we need to have the nothing option available to us all the time.

Despite its significant advantages over other methods, win-win has a great disadvantage: it cannot be imposed by force on the other side. It can only be adopted voluntarily. That's why at the beginning of any meaningful relationship, the parties must have a serious discussion about its nature and on what principles to conduct it.

REMEMBER: EFFECTIVE RELATIONSHIPS ARE
ALWAYS BASED ON TRUST AND MUTUAL BENEFITS

The Art of Influencing Others

"In the beginning was the Word, and the Word was with God, and the Word was God." (John 1:1)

On Influence

In one of the previous chapters, we discussed about the Circle of Influence. Let's now examine together how it applies to influence people and events.

Influencing people simply means that I can convince them to do what I desire them to do. Influencing events means I have the power to push things in a specific direction or to oppose them going there. The more people you have under your influence, the better chances you have to shape events. Let's take a couple of historical examples. Spartacus, a gladiator in Roman times, became the leader of many other slaves fighting for freedom. He thus threatened the very foundation of the Roman empire. Martin Luther, the religious activist of 16th century Europe, influenced millions of people with his call for reforming the Catholic church. The Protestant church was born from his actions.

Life consists of scores of influences every day that help us mold into the persons we are. As J.C. Maxwell (b.1959) puts it: *"No one can understand the mysterious thing we call influence...yet every one of us continually exerts it to heal, to bless, or to leave a mark of beauty, or to wound, to hurt, or poison other lives."*[101] This truth should sober us, because it states the considerable impact we as parents have on our children. The issue is not whether you influence someone; the problem is what kind of influence you will be: a good or a bad one. This is the fundamental question. The capacity to influence others is also found in the so-called triangle of power.[102] The triangle of power starts with effective communication, which leads to recognition by others, which in turn leads to influence over others. And this creates enormous power.

To conclude, we can safely say that influence is the primary attribute of leadership. Once you influence people, they will follow you. Think of great leaders like Jesus of Nazareth, Mahatma Gandhi, and John F. Kennedy. What did they have in common? Lots of followers!

On Verbal Communications

Let's now have a glimpse into the art and science of human communications. There is no doubt that communications play a vital role in human life. They not only facilitate the process of sharing information, but also help people to develop relationships with each other. Every day, we communicate with a lot of people, including our families, friends, colleagues, or even strangers. Learning to communicate effectively will, for sure, make our lives better.

> **Wherefore, my beloved brethren,**
> **let every man be swift to hear,**
> **slow to speak, slow to wrath.**
> **James 1:19**

Verbal communications use spoken words. From the dawn of humanity, the word has had a special meaning and significance in all civilizations. For instance, in Christianity, the Word has been equated to God. In modern linguistics, the word is the smallest element that may be spoken or written in isolation and have a meaning. Therefore, the word is the building block of messages, which are constructs designed to convey information, thoughts, and feelings.

Information is any entity that provides the answer to a question of some kind. The concept of information is a profound one, rooted in mathematics, central to whole branches of science, yet with direct implications in every aspect of our lives. Related to information is the concept of meaning, which is the abstract thought carried by the information transmitted by a message.

Verbal Messages

Now, let's look a bit closer at what happens when you and I are having a conversation together. Say I want to send you some new information about something. To do this, I have to create a message and speak it to you. At your end, you will have to hear my words and interpret them. As I begin to create my message, the information in my head is being shaped by three powerful forces. The first is my mentality, the second is my attitude towards you, and the third is my ability to compose the message. Let's try to understand what's going on.

To start with, I have my own ideas and feelings about the subject matter. Therefore, when I try to formulate the message for you, my mindset will influence its structure and presentation. Besides, a second psychological filter, i.e., my attitude towards you, will come into play. If I respect you, I will choose words compatible with this attitude, and my voice will be soft. But if I don't, I may use words harsher or less respectful, and the voice will definitely show my disregard for you. And thirdly, I have to put my message in words and organize it in sentences. That depends a lot on my language skills. If I am a proficient speaker, my message will be clear, short, and simple to understand. In contrast, if my language skills are lacking, my talk will tend to be longer, confusing, and for sure, more difficult to comprehend.

Once I speak, my words will travel through the air as sound waves. The intensity and quality of the sound waves reaching your ears will depend on how loud my voice is, the distance between the two of us, and the noise perturbations around us. For instance, you may not hear all my words properly, or you may have them mixed up. For this reason, there will be at least a small amount of distortion in the information traveling from me to you.

When my words reach your ears, they convert into nervous impulses, which in turn get to your brain. In there, they are decoded, analyzed, and interpreted to recreate the message. And above all, to extract its intended meaning. Once again, these cerebral activities are done in accordance with your mentality, your attitude towards me, and your language skills. For example, if you are suspicious of me, you will be very guarded and skeptical when interpreting my message. In contrast, if we are close friends and have known each other for a long time, your interpretation will be made with ease and plenty of goodwill. Equally important, if you are not a good wordsmith, you will tend to be wary about the words I use.

The bottom line is this: the original information in my head becomes altered information in yours due to distortions. Equally so, the higher-level meaning of that message is also changed. The changes can be minor or major, depending on how far apart our mentalities are, what attitudes we have toward one another, the proficiency in language usage, and the quality of the transmission channel.

REMEMBER: INFORMATION AND ITS MEANING
CONTAINED IN VERBAL MESSAGES WILL
ALWAYS BE DISTORTED BY PSYCHOLOGICAL
AND ENVIRONMENTAL REASONS

Non-verbal Components of Messages

When we talk face- to- face, besides your words, I also hear the speed, rhythm, and cadence of your speech, the inflection of your voice, the sounds made by your breathing. I also see your body language as well: how you sit, how you gesture, how you hold your head, how you look at me, if you lean toward me or away from me. This is the unspoken language of the message, which, together with the spoken words, convey to me a complex emotional-rational message.

There is a compelling body of research on the relative importance of verbal and nonverbal messages.[103] When considering the tone of voice and body language alongside the spoken words, researchers have found that the three elements may account differently in our overall reception of the message: words account for a small percentage, the voice for a larger, and the body language for an even larger one. These findings lead to an indisputable conclusion: in face-to-face communications, the tone of voice and body language are as important as the spoken words.

Dialogue

The most common way of speaking among people is called dialogue, talk, chat, or conversation. Dialogue happens when two or more people exchange information, ideas, and emotions. We conduct discussions every day in the family, at work, with friends. Most times, the dialogues are on routine matters such as daily activities, work topics or family issues, etc. But in special cases, the conversation deals with important, sensitive, and emotional issues between people. As such, it becomes a higher-level dialogue. In a high-level discussion, we seek to set aside fears, preconceptions, and the need to win. And we take time to hear other voices, ask questions, and provide answers to understand each other better.

One of the most notable effects of a high-level dialogue is the mutual influence it offers to all participants. Not only you acquire more knowledge by listening to new ideas, but you also start to know better, at both intellectual and emotional levels, the people you converse with. Look back at dialogues in your past, after which you told yourself: *"My goodness, I thought I knew that person well, but during our recent conversation, she had exceeded all my expectations."* We all have experienced similar situations, which means they are universal.

One last observation about dialogues: quite a few of them fail. Why is that? Because of the use of accusatory language, sarcastic remarks, inquisitional questioning, losing temper, and so on. You must avoid them at all costs. If the other party is using them, first try to deflect them, then call attention to their detrimental effect on the conversation. If it doesn't work, stand up and walk away right then and there, because this kind of dialogue only wastes your time.

Dialogue of the Deaf

We all know how most conversations go: everybody wants to speak, but nobody wants to listen. Very few think that listening is really necessary, and even fewer have the patience to do it. Why should they? Everyone looks at a dialogue as a contest between two points of view, rather than an exchange of rational thoughts and personal feelings. And in a match, you must fight to win. Isn't it so? As a result, most dialogues taking place between humans can be called "dialogue of the deaf."[104]

Let's see what goes through my head almost at a subconscious level during such a dialogue with you. First of all, the important thing for me is only my point of view, not yours. I am not talking to you to hear your opinion, but for you to listen to mine. For this reason, I rush to speak first to ensure that my point of view is known early, so I conquer the territory on which the dialogue will take place.

When your turn comes to speak, I pretend to listen, but in fact, I prepare my rebuttal. I do not want to hear your point of view. In fact, I am not interested in it. Why should I be? I know my point of view is right. Therefore, this conversation is only an opportunity to fight tooth and nail to defend my position, to prove my point, to demonstrate I am the smartest.

Aren't we all aware of this way of thinking before a dialogue even begins? Aren't we all guilty of using it numerous times in the past? We could never explain why talks carried this way all fail and take the relationship down the drain with them. But this is the harsh reality: the dialogue of the deaf is common everywhere, even though it is a big letdown. It does not bring any better understanding of each other, nor does it provide a solution to the issue at hand. It is just a waste of time and a source of anguish and frustration. Is this an effective way to communicate? You'll be the judge!

The Golden Rule of Effective Communications

The key to effective communications has been brilliantly summed up by Dr. Stephen Covey (1932-2012) in one sentence:[105] *"seek first to understand, then to be understood"*. In other words: listen first, talk second.

Put it in other words: Listen with your heart first; talk with passion after. Let's call it the Golden Rule of effective communications. If you adopt this simple yet powerful rule – to see things from another's point of view first –a whole new world of excitement will open up for you.

LISTEN WITH YOUR HEART FIRST.
TALK WITH PASSION AFTER

Why is the Golden Rule the key to effective communication? It's because the most profound need of any human being is to be understood. Since early times, everyone wanted to be respected and valued for who they are: a unique, one-of-a-kind individual. To open up to you, people need to know first that you appreciate, value, and care about them. And how do you show that you care? By trying hard to understand the other person at the most profound level possible. Have you heard the saying: *"People don't care how much you know until they know how much you care"*? So true. Think about a situation in the past when someone did not take the time to listen and understand you. Were you open to what they had to say? Of course not, because your subconscious mind was telling you, *"If she does not care about me, why should I care about her words?"*

Listen with Your Heart

Listening with the heart is called 'empathic listening.' It is also known as in-depth listening, total listening, or perceptive listening.[106] Empathic listening is much more than active hearing: it involves an awareness of what is being said verbally and nonverbally, as well as what is not being said. It perceives not only with the ears, but also with the eyes; not only with the mind, but also with the heart. Empathic listening, both relationally and spiritually, is strenuous and challenging work. It is aptly described in these terms *"The act of listening requires a submersion of the self and immersion in the other . . . Learning to listen involves a paradox of control: controlling yourself and letting go of control of the relationship. It is like letting the other person drive. To listen, you have to let go"*. Why the need to listen so deeply? Because only there can I find your mentality, your outlook on life, your unconscious you. Only there may I uncover your hidden emotions and feelings, your vulnerabilities and strengths.

Now, going that deep is not easy. As a matter of fact, it is very hard. Why is this the case? Because for me to enter into your frame of mind, into your paradigm, I have to leave mine outside. For me to walk into your shoes, I have to remove mine first. For me to understand your heart, I must find the key to unlock it so I can see what's inside. Empathic listening is difficult because it requires unusual sensitivity, knowledge, skills, and sensitivity on my part. Empathic listening is hard because it requires patience, effort, time, and perhaps the right circumstances for the dialogue. Empathic listening does not imply agreement. It merely means that I am committed to deep listening, even when I do not agree with what you're saying. I do not judge you. I do not criticize. I do not praise you. I just listen. I try to be just a neutral observer of your soul.

Dialogues in which partners listen with their hearts are also named heart-to-heart dialogues. This expression is used when describing a deep and intimate conversation between two individuals, often of the opposite sex.[107] Opening up our hearts to close friends provides sublime feelings of satisfaction, friendship, and love. Holding hands, looking into each other's eyes, leaning towards each other, using soft voices, and shedding an occasional tear, enhance the emotional connection between the parties. It becomes part of the magic that takes place during a heart-to-heart talk. Also, heart-to-heart dialogue is the most effective means of understanding the other person deeply, and to influence her in a positive way.

Seek to be Understood

Seek first to understand...then to be understood. Knowing how to be understood is the other half of the Golden Rule in communications, and it is equally critical in reaching Win-Win solutions. Listening with your heart helps you empathize with the other's point of view. Now is time for you to talk and make sure the other party identifies with yours.

REMEMBER: THE KEY TO OPENING ONE'S
HEART IS TO LISTEN TO ONE'S HEART

The ancient Greeks had a marvelous way of thinking about speech embodied in three words: *ethos, pathos,* and *logos.*[108] These three words must be in sequence and make the essence of making an effective speech. They provide the key to the art of persuasion.

- *Ethos* is your personal credibility, the faith that people have in your integrity and competency. It's the trust that you inspire, your relational bank account.
- *Pathos* is the empathic side - it's the feelings. It means that you are in contact with the emotional drive of the other party's communication.
- *Logos* is the logic, the reasoning part of the presentation.

Notice the sequence: ethos, pathos, and logos - your character comes first, second your emotional connection, and third the logic of your argument. Let's call it the Enchanted Sequence. It represents another major paradigm shift from contemporary culture. Most people jump straight to the logos, trying to show people their rational arguments without first bringing ethos and pathos into the picture. They start a direct attack without first softening the defenses. No wonder that few succeed.

When you present your thoughts plainly, and with a deep concern for your audience's needs, you significantly increase the credibility of your arguments. The viewers sense right away that you are not wrapped into your ego. You are not delivering grandiose rhetoric just to feed your vanity. They sense that presenting with conviction ideas in which you believe, taking all known facts and perceptions into consideration, you genuinely want to benefit all of them.

The Enchanted Sequence

Let's look closer now at how the enchanted sequence will help you organize and order your response during a two-parties dialogue, say with a trusted friend. Since you trust each other, your answer doesn't need to start with ethos; it can go straight to pathos, then to logos.

1. You acknowledge respect for his point of view, emphasizing its merits and highlighting what you particularly like about it.

2. You express appreciation of the underlying desires and emotions behind his point of view, accepting their validity.

3. You require clarification on some aspects of his position, both on the emotional and rational side.

4. You point to topics that separate the two points of view and commit to working with him to solving them based on acceptable principles.

5. Now it's time to start making your logical arguments. First, you acknowledge that his arguments have influenced your thoughts, which currently differ from your original ideas. You present your arguments with conviction and passion, highlight their benefits. You constantly watch for your interlocutor's body language and gauge your talking accordingly.

6. You conclude by stating your commitment to blending the two original ideas into something better, into a new synergistic solution that both of us will like better and benefit greatly. You invite him to work together to find the magic Win-Win that will make both of you happy.

> REMEMBER: THE PURPOSE OF YOUR RESPONSE IS TO CONVINCE THE OTHER PARTY TO JOIN UP IN SEARCHING FOR A NEW WIN-WIN SOLUTION

Speak with Passion

Now that your turn has come to speak, how do you achieve maximum impact on the audience? There is a large body of knowledge in this field and many examples of great, compelling speakers. What they have in common, experts agree, are outstanding skills in preparation of the speech as well as in its delivery.

Speech preparation involves researching the topic, structuring the presentation, practicing, knowing your audience, and familiarizing yourself with the venue. And last but not least, get excited before stepping on stage.

Good speakers are passionate - and it shows. Bad speakers are dull - and it shows. Good speakers are animated by their material, and their positive energy goes a long way toward winning over listeners. Why is that? Simply because people like positive energy, they are attracted to it. They want to be around good motivators who put all their heart into what they tell them.

Here are several ingredients for compelling, passionate, yet rational communications that apply in all situations: one-on-one dialogue, talking to a small group, or speaking from a podium.[109]

1. **Make your message vibrant and colorful**: Passion tells your audience that you're fully invested in what you're talking about. Your feelings are on full display to prove it.

2. **Add deliberate movements and gestures**: These will visibly engage your audience and become the most visible dimension of your body language, particularly when you're on stage. Walking, changing your pace, even jumping up and down, taking a well-timed step toward your audience, or a convincing hand gesture will add impact to what you're saying.

3. **Use a powerful voice**: The voice of passionate speakers captures and mesmerizes the audience. Let's face it: when you speak, your voice captivates or puts them to sleep. Your voice should be robust and intense, reflecting your emotions and confidence in what you're saying. Power does not necessarily mean high volume - you can have a quiet intensity in your voice.

4. **Add dimension:** The voice should follow the peaks and valleys of your message by mounting crescendos, then dropping down to consolidate meaning. It is about the way you sound - not necessarily

the tone of your voice. Use a higher rhythm to build anticipation, followed by a more relaxed pace after you made your point.

5. **Make your audience laugh:** Tell relevant, funny stories about yourself to make your audience laugh. Laughter is the surest way to connect with people, and the easiest way to open to them up emotionally. When people are relaxed, smile, or laugh, their brains are ready to absorb new information. They learn best when they feel positive emotions.

6. **Maintain clarity:** Despite speaking passionately, your points should still flow logically from one to the next. Maintain the essential quality of your message - its clarity. Make sure you always emphasize the main idea you want to get across.

The Wonders of Mutual Influence

Let's go back to the topic of a heart-to-heart dialogue. As we've seen above, during such an intimate conversation, you open your heart to me so I can better understand your hidden feelings. But the question becomes: can I stay neutral as I listen to your heart? And the surprising yet firm answer is no. I cannot remain indifferent as my own heart understands deeper and deeper the cries of your own. Why does this happen? Because in its essence, the human nature is good, being a reflection of the divine nature of our Creator. I cannot remain indifferent to what I see in your heart; my heart begins to feel your pain. I cannot stay indifferent to your cry for help; my heart compels me to act.

Besides, other crucial psychological fact takes place.[110] As I start influencing you because your heart is open and ready to listen, the reciprocal also becomes true. You start affecting me as well, at least in some measure. In other words, the wonder of mutual influence starts working its magic on both of us. Using empathic listening signifies not only my sincere desire to read and understand your heart, but my willingness to open mine for your inspection as well. Both hearts are prepared for the marvels of mutual influence, which is the essence of a meaningful relationship.

And here comes the dilemma: Is it a good thing to be influenced by you, or is it a bad thing? On the one hand, I might be afraid to be affected because I don't want to change. I like the way I am. On the other hand, if the price to influencing you is to be, to some extent, being influenced by you, why not accept it? Christian teachings tell us that the latter is the right way to go and that mutual influence is the unavoidable yet highly desirable result of heart-to-heart conversations.

Unfortunately, the worldly culture maintains that being influenceable means to be weak. While this may be true for many, it is not valid for people of Diamond Soul character. A man of integrity is steadfast in his principles yet flexible in methods. He is not afraid of changes because he is sure about the changeless nature of his beliefs. A person of character is not worried about opening up his soul and becoming vulnerable. When being influenced by others, people of character do not change their value principles; they only seek solutions to a particular problem and are prepared to change their methods.

Empathic listening requires lots of courage on my part. However, as a man of character, I accept your influence only if it changes my view about the issue under discussion. I will never accept any attempts to change my character or the principles on which it is based. In return, however, I should expect that you, too, will change your current view about the issue at hand. It is this mutual influence that will allow us to seek a new, higher solution to our problem. Therefore, mutual influence is the first step toward making our dialogue useful.

REMEMBER: WHEN INFLUENCING YOU, I
AM BEING INFLUENCED BY YOU TOO

The Art of Creative Cooperation

"Two are better than one, because they have a good reward for their labor"

(Ecclesiastes 4:8-12)

Creative cooperation consists of valuing the difference between people, using the power of synergy, and thinking outside the box. Cooperating creatively is an art, same as listening and speaking are arts. Mastering this art for the benefit of many is the crown jewel of all other principles studied so far.

<u>Differences</u>

Differences between humans is a magnificent property given to us by our Creator. Differences lead to diversity, and diversity leads to uniqueness. We are all unique in so many ways, but is uniqueness good or bad? On the one hand, we can look at it as a barrier between people, and in many cases, it is indeed. On the other, if we learn how to use it properly, it will open new worlds before us.

In this material, we will look at differences as the qualities that make one person unlike another. This means that the total of your personal qualities makes you different from other people. These qualities include physical appearance, psychological makeup (temperament), moral character, spirituality, aptitudes, and skills. In popular culture, the differences between people are often portrayed as the source of mistrust and conflict between them. Unfortunately, human history confirms that this is the case. Someone who looks and speaks differently from me becomes therefore suspicious, mistrustful, and even threatening. I have to be extra careful, because they do not belong to the same clan as me, and this violates the natural order of 'birds of same feather flock together.' But it doesn't have to be that way! Differences, although exposing what is obviously dissimilar between us, may also hide what can take us to a higher level of understanding.

Diversity

Diversity in a group is created by differences between the members of that group. When we see a group of women wearing clothes of various colors and speaking in multiple tongues, we say that the group is diverse. In contrast, when we see a group of soldiers all dresses the same and marching in lockstep, we say that the group is uniform. Diversity and uniformity are opposites, but each has a distinct role in the society.

The concept of diversity must encompass acceptance and respect. It means understanding that each individual is unique and recognizing our individual differences. These can be along the dimensions of race, ethnicity, gender, socio-economic status, age, physical abilities, religious beliefs, political beliefs, or other ideologies. Diversity implies the exploration of these differences in a safe, positive, and nurturing environment.[111]

Diversity also refers to differences in language, tradition, and values. This kind of diversity is called cultural diversity. Cultural norms have historically separated societies that emerged around the globe, and many of these differences persist to this day. However, in the modern era of globalization, when people travel a lot and move from one place to another in search of work or a better life, the cultural differences become more and more apparent. Just look around you; you are surrounded by people slightly different, modestly different, or strikingly different than you. In this blessed country of ours, where most people have different ethnic backgrounds, we grow up seeing, accepting, and valuing diversity. Yet, when we are to face it, most of us have no clue how to handle it. Therefore, we must learn.

Why are We so Unique?

It is easier to understand the differences when we recognize that we are all unique and distinct individuals. In other words, we are all a minority of one. There are 330 million minorities of one in the U.S., and you and I are just two of them! The uniqueness of our personality is not only on the surface - how we look, speak, or dress - but also deep inside us. Everyone has their way of thinking and their own outlook on life.

Let's outline the primary reasons we are so unique:

We have different genes. This is, for sure, the foundational difference. Genes not only makes us look different, but they endow our bodies and minds with unlike characteristics.

We are born with different temperaments. Temperament is the psychological makeup you are born with. Therefore, it is also pre-programmed in your genes. Temperament refers to those aspects of an individual's personality that are regarded as biologically based, rather than learned.

We come from different backgrounds. Families in which we were born and raised provided a developmental environment unique to each family. The education we get at an early age, in school, or college is critical to our further intellectual development.

We learn differently. Individual learning styles have more influence than people may realize. They not only define the way you learn, but also change the way you internally represent experiences, the way you recall information, and even the words you choose.

Our Moral Character is Different. When it comes to the concept of moral character, some people have no idea what it means, while others have their morality float with circumstances. On the other hand, the readers of this book, and perhaps others work hard to build a robust moral character, the same as Jesus Christ's.

Spirituality. Our spirituality is different. Some people have no concept of God at all, others refuse to acknowledge a divine authority, and still others may belong to different religious traditions.

We think and see things differently. We all have psychological filters deeply engrained in our being, which determine how we see, think, and act. In a sense, they define who we are. It goes to show that all events of your past have formed a unique prism through which you see the world. We cannot say that you are better or worse than me; we can only acknowledge we are unlike.

Respecting the Uniqueness of Individuals

Respecting the uniqueness of people is the secret to a superior way of interaction, understanding, and cooperation between them. Why is it this way? Because being unique and different from one another is a divine gift from the Almighty, and when used correctly, it draws us close to him. The very essence of humanity, its assurance for perpetual existence on Earth, is the difference between sexes. By making the man and woman purposely different from one another but one in the flesh, God has reproduced in them the divine unity that the triune God himself is. Each sex is distinct and valuable, and both reflect the image and likeness of God.

> **Two are better than one;**
> **because they have**
> **a good reward for their labour.**
> **Ecclesiastes 4:8**

Appreciating the differences means first to recognize and respect them, to build on strength, to compensate for weaknesses. Valuing the differences means to use them to create synergy, the highest level of dealings between people. This is particularly true about the differences not immediately apparent, mostly those related to the makeup of the inner self. They can include intellectual, emotional, and spiritual differences; or variances related to temperament, skills, and inclinations. Could these differences become a source for creating something new, something exciting, and unseen before? Of course, they could, as we shall see further down where we learn about cooperating at a higher level, the synergetic level. But for this to happen, we must learn to step out of our comfort zone. It means to start thinking out of the box.

Synergy

A simple definition of synergy states that "the whole is greater than the sum of all its parts." Words having the same meaning as synergy are cooperation, joint action, collaboration, and symbiotic relationship.[112]

Theoretically, we can say that synergy is found at the intersection of three circles: the circle of differences, the circle of thinking outside the box, and the circle of open communications. Let's explain: if the two of us have differences we want resolved (first circle), we have to think in an original manner (second circle) and communicate openly and sincerely (third circle) with one another. In practice, synergy can occur only if I have a great relationship with you, I bring a mentality of abundance, and I think win-win. In other words, I am a person of character who cares about you, I believe there is enough for both of us out there, and I'm willing to share it with you. Each of us individually can achieve only so much, as expressed by the simple arithmetic formula: I + YOU = 2. However, if we add the synergistic relationship between the two of us, the equation becomes: I + YOU + RELATIONSHIP = 3. Now, this is synergistic!

By thinking outside the box, we create new alternatives - something that wasn't there before. We create new ways of interacting. It stimulates, unifies, and releases the greatest power within people. All we have learned so far in this book prepares us to enter into the beautiful world of synergy and creative collaboration. But this world is also scary because you do not know what's going to happen and where it is going to lead. You don't know what new slippery slopes and roadblocks you'll encounter. It will require a great amount of internal security and personal courage on your part to do it. In other words, you have to be a person of Diamond Soul character to be able to accomplish it. But in doing so, you become an explorer, a vanguard, a trailblazer. You open new horizons and lands so that others can follow.

Synergy in Humans, God, and Nature.

As we know, human beings are created in the image of the triune God. As such, the human psyche is complex and nearly incomprehensible. We are body, mind, emotions, and spirit – four entities working in harmony with one another to define a unique person. When it comes to God's triune nature, how much more complex and beyond our finite ability to understand is his makeup? The Bible teaches us that God comprises three distinct entities: God the Father, God the Son, and God the Spirit. Our difficulty is that while God is one and God is three, he is one in a different way than he is three.

In the natural world, synergistic phenomena are found everywhere, ranging from cooperative interactions among genes in genomes, to divisions of labor in bacterial colonies, to the synergies of scale in multi-cellular organisms, and so on. Synergy is also found in socially organized groups, from honeybee colonies, to wolf packs, to bird flocks.

Synergy in Human Society

Human synergy relates to human cooperation and teamwork. For example, let's say Alice alone is too short to reach a high object, and brother John is not tall enough, either. However, once John lifts his sister, they together can touch the desired object.

When used in a business setting, synergy means that teamwork will produce an overall better result than the sum of individual efforts. It follows that a synergistic group is more than the sum of its parts. When used in a technical context, synergy becomes synonymous with the system. System means a collection of different elements working together to produce results not obtainable by any of the items alone. The components can include people, hardware, software, facilities, policies, and documents. They all are the necessary things required to produce a synergistic system-level result. The value added by the system as a whole, beyond that contributed independently by the parts, is created primarily by the relationship among its components. That is, how they are interconnected.[113] Smartphones are the best example of a highly synergistic system that blends micro-electronics, optics, telecommunications, software, and emerging artificial intelligence to create a miracle of technology.

<u>The Third Alternative</u>

The essence of the art of creative cooperation is searching for a new way: not mine, not yours but a higher one, like the apex of a triangle. It is also called the third alternative or the higher way. Searching for the third alternative implies that you have bought into the idea that differences are a strength, not a weakness, and you, therefore, respect diversity. But how do you actually look for it? How do you go about it? Here is the answer: follow the five-step action plan shown below.

Define the Problem/Opportunity: Here, you need to listen empathically to others' ideas and do your best to understand it. Ask questions, require clarifications, look deeper into the underlying emotions or wishes to Their way. Do not denigrate it. Do not criticize it. Just listen to it.

My Way: Now it is your turn to speak. State what you like and what you don't about their way. Express your respect for the intentions and emotions beyond it. Then, describe your ideas with clarity and passion; emphasize why they are so dear to you. Explain your feelings and emotions behind your proposed way. Then, state that you are willing to search for a better way to satisfy both parties.

Brainstorm: Moderate a respectful and sincere brainstorming session during which new options and alternatives are created, laid down on the table, and discussed. They are no longer your ideas, they are no longer their ideas, but they are the new ideas resulting from the collective effort. During the brainstorming process, do not criticize any alternative, do not shut any down, do not embrace any too early. Just expose them to a thorough and in-depth review.

The Third Alternative. Slowly, as the brainstorming process takes its ups and downs, a new alternative is starting to surface. You will recognize it because it will appeal to you and the other party as well. When you're close to it, the excitement starts to rise, and everyone will want to talk about it. Once the third alternative has been found, your job is to reformulate it for the last time with clarity and enthusiasm. And, finally, to get everyone's nod of approval, and shake hands over it.

The Synergizer

The synergizer is a man of Diamond Soul character with a talent for creative cooperation and a humble attitude. As Dr. Stephen R. Covey puts it, the fundamental approach of the synergizer towards their interlocutor is: *"if a person of your competence and commitment disagrees with me, then there must be something that I don't get. You must have a perspective I need to look at and understand. Please help me achieve that!"*[114]

The key to interpersonal synergy is the intra-personal synergy, that is, synergy internal to our self. The heart of internal synergy is embodied in the Diamond Soul character, which provides the internal security to handle the risks of being open and vulnerable. Only a Diamond Soul character allows us to develop the abundance mentality of win-win, and the sincerity and power of synergy. The synergizer has the humility to recognize his limitations and appreciate the richness discovered through interaction with other human beings. The synergizer values the differences because they add to his knowledge, and to his understanding of reality.

> REMEMBER: ONLY A PERSON OF HIGH INTEGRITY AND DEEP HUMILITY CAN BECOME A SYNERGIZER

Are you ready to turn the page? If yes, go right ahead to see what new facets you are going to add to your Diamond Soul character. Those facets will help you preserve and enhance the greatest asset you have. You will be surprised to find out what that asset is!

Moments of Reflection

1. In a quiet place, reflect on how you've been dealing with people around you so far: were you fair to them? Did you think of their needs? Did you strive for equity in relationships?
2. What is trust? What is mutual interest?
3. What is a relational bank account? Provide examples of deposits and withdrawals in an RBA.
4. What is the win-lose matrix? Describe the strategies in managing human relations based on the four possible outcomes
5. Why win-win or nothing is considered the best strategy?
6. What is influence?
7. What are verbal messages? Describe how they are created, transmitted, and received.

8. What is a distorted message?

9. What is the golden rule of verbal communications?

10. What is empathic listening?

11. Why should you speak with passion?

12. What is the enchanted sequence?

13. What is mutual influence? Which are its effects on participants?

14. Why are we so unique as individuals?

15. What is synergy? Provide an example of synergistic behavior in human society and nature

16. What is the third alternative?

17. Which are the traits of a synegizer?

CHAPTER 18
DAILY REJUVENATION

"… What? know ye not that your body is the temple of
the Holy Ghost which is in you, which ye have of God,
and ye are not your own? (1 Corinthians 6:19-20)

This is the story about daily rejuvenation told by Cathy Jacobs, co-founder of Fire Inside Leadership:[115]

"The first great aha for me in my own journey back to balance was when I finally understood that balance is an inside job. That realization came when I decided to leave my demanding 24/7 job and start working for myself. After radically changing my external circumstances, within a few months of starting my own business, I found myself right back where I was before I left – working 12 to 16-hour days, exhausted and overwhelmed. Finally, facing that the common denominator in this situation was me, was both painful and empowering.

The second shift came more slowly. It was the realization that balance is an act of recovery. Recovering to balance has been a process of experimentation – of making continuous small adjustments back to a sense of equilibrium. This process of experimentation was not an act of will, but the incorporation of a number of small habits and rituals in my life to support me to live the way I want to live."

This chapter deals with renewing yourself on a daily basis. Rejuvenating implies taking care of the most valuable asset you have - You. Yes, this is right; you are your most important asset. It is not your job; it is not your house, nor is it your bank account. It is you, your health, your intellect, your emotions, and your soul. Without your health, you cannot function; without your brain, you cannot reason; without your feelings, you are not you; and without your soul, you are spiritually dead. All these four dimensions defined you in the past, make you who you are today, and will set you in the future. Therefore, you must take outstanding care of them.

The Significance of Daily Rejuvenation

Daily rejuvenation has a tremendous Christian significance because it follows numerous teachings about the body, mind, heart, and spirit found in the Bible. Here is just one of them:

"But the wisdom that is from above is first pure, then peaceable, gentle, *and* easy to be intreated, full of mercy and good fruits, without partiality, and without hypocrisy." (James 3:17)

Daily Rejuvenation puts in practice the teachings of all stepping stones learned so far. Without Daily Rejuvenation, the great treasure of robust conceptional and practical knowhow found in this book remains just that - good conceptual knowledge. But as is the case with any knowhow, if it's not reviewed regularly and rehearsed every day, it will fade away and eventually disappears. And all your efforts in acquiring it would have been in vain. You should not allow this to happen!

Daily renewal is your most important daily activity because:

- It preserves, strengthens, and enhances the greatest asset you have - you.
- It refreshes all principles learned in this material, and lets you practice and experiment with them until they get fully internalized.
- It brings them alive in a holistic and harmonious you of body, intellect, emotions, and spirit.
- It makes your new Diamond Soul character shine and inspire others.
- It lets you serve God and fellowmen in more effective ways.

To do all these activities regularly, you must be proactive. Daily Rejuvenation is a definite Quadrant II activity; it is maintenance and prevention at its best. Daily self-renewal must be pressed upon from an early age until it becomes second nature, fully internalized and operational almost at an unconscious level. By its very nature, no one else can do the daily self-renewal for you. You must do it yourself by using self-discipline and willpower in a wise and balanced way.

> REMEMBER: CARING FOR YOURSELF IS THE SINGLE MOST IMPORTANT INVESTMENT YOU CAN MAKE

Caring for Body and Health

Caring for your body means eating right, getting physical exercise, and resting enough.

Practical Advice on Nutrition.

There is so much truth to the expression, "You are what you eat." If you overeat junk food, sooner or later, your body will become a junk body. On the other hand, if you eat healthy food, your body will stay healthy. In today's America, we see the disturbing results of decades of unhealthy eating habits and poor nutrition. The time has come for the new generation of Americans to turn things around!

Poor eating habits include overeating or consuming too many types of junk food and drinks, which are low in fiber or high in fat, salt, and sugar. Poor nutrition can impair our well-being and reduce our ability to lead an enjoyable and active life. In the short term, a poor diet can contribute to stress, lack of energy, and tiredness. Over time, it increases the risk of developing health problems such as obesity, tooth decay, high blood pressure, diabetes, depression, etc.

The key to healthy nutrition is variety, balance, and moderation. Our bodies need a daily intake of protein, carbohydrates, essential fatty acids, vitamins, and minerals, as well as fiber and fluids. Take a look at the MyPlate nutritional guidelines issued by the U.S. Department of Agriculture.[116] You will see a plate divided into four sections of approximately 30 percent grains, 40 percent vegetables, 10 percent fruits, and 20 percent protein, accompanied by a smaller circle representing dairy, such as a glass of milk or a yogurt cup.

Which are the common-sense rules for proper nutrition?

- Eat foods based on a healthy diet plan every day.
- Drink at least six glasses of clean water instead of sodas or juices.
- Plan your meals ahead and shop for healthy ingredients.
- Enjoy cooking and eating healthy food with family or friends.
- Use alcohol only on social occasions and in moderation.

Foods to consume only occasionally, or to avoid altogether if possible: red meat, processed food of any kind, pizzas, white bread and pastas. Stay away from French fries, potato chips, pastries, candy bars, ice cream, sodas, and sugary drinks. Avoid animal fat, coffee, and salt.

Besides using good food, you should also follow these common-sense rules: have the main meals at the same time during the day, eat in moderation, take small but healthy snacks between meals, and drink plenty of water. What about drugs? A big no-no!

Practical Advice on Physical Exercise

Do you remember the movie, Forrest Gump? When frustrated and puzzled about his existence, Forrest starts running back and forth from one coast to another, until he decides he has had enough. This story, although bizarre, tells a fundamental truth: physical exercise is a necessary condition for human existence, and the best way to maintain health.

We all occasionally feel depressed, apathetic, and confused. When this happens, take proactive corrective measures right away: go for a walk, jog or swim, plan a weekend at the beach or in the hills, and so on. Exercise is not only good for your heart, muscles, and lungs, but it will melt stress away and refresh your mind. There are many ways to stay fit. Some people run, walk, swim, do yoga, or lift weights. Still others, just like to go outside for a stroll, walk the dogs, or simply enjoy a breath of fresh air.

Exercise is a Quadrant II activity that most people don't do all the time because it is not urgent. And because we don't do it, sooner or later, we find ourselves in Quadrant I, dealing with medical problems that come as a result of our neglect. Unfortunately, most of us think we do not have enough time to exercise. What a mistake! Think about the tremendous benefits a half-hour of exercise will bring to the rest of the day: better productivity, better mood, better sleep!

A good exercise program is one you do in your own home, and builds strength, endurance, and flexibility. If you want to go to the gym or practice high-intensity sports such as tennis, basketball, or hockey, that is a bonus, and you should enjoy it. A balanced in-home daily exercise program should last 30 to 45 minutes and be done early in the morning. It should include warming up, stretching, aerobics, strength building, and cooling down. If you want, you can add some elements of yoga, particularly those postures related to improving balance, flexibility, and breathing. While exercising, keep windows open to get fresh air in the room. If the weather is cooperating, do your morning fitness program outdoors, and definitely include a ten-minute jogging session.[117]

One final relevant comment about maintaining your health: you can only do so much on your own; from time to time, you need professional help. Make it a routine to visit your doctor for annual checkups. Keep him informed on how you eat and sleep, and what fitness program you're following. If you fall sick, get medical attention right away - remember this is a Quadrant I crisis, it must be addressed with urgency! Otherwise, it will only get worse.

Practical Advice on Sleeping

Along with nutrition and exercise, good sleep is one of the pillars of health. Resting your body means giving it enough hours of sleep every night and taking perhaps a short nap during the day. We are all different, and our bodies have distinctive sleeping and resting needs. Studies show that, on average, most people are satisfied with 7–8 hours per night. The benefits of a good night's sleep are well known and documented: boosts physical performance, increases various brain functions such as cognition, concentration, memory, enhances immune system operation, makes you alert and energetic, and so on. Besides, it improves your emotional and social life as well as decreases the risks of diseases.

Other healthy tips: go to bed and get up at the same hour, eat your last meal of the day about three hours before going to bed, and get some quiet time reading or relaxing before turning your lights off. Your bedroom should be adequately heated and ventilated. In winter, a humidifier improves the relative humidity in the room, which will help you sleep better. In summer, leave your windows open to get fresh air.[118]

> REMEMBER: NOW YOU HAVE THE KNOWHOW
> AND SELF-DISCIPLINE TO EAT
> HEALTHY AND STAY FIT.
> GO DO IT!

Caring for Brain, Mind, and Intellect

Caring for your brain, mind, and intellect means enhancing brainpower through education, reading, watching instructional videos, learning hobbies, and doing mind-sharpening activities. Caring for your brain also means staying informed, interested, and engaged in what's going on locally, nationally, and in the world.

Practical Advice on Caring for Your Brain

At every stage in your life, you want your brain to improve its mental acuity and memory. Unfortunately, the peak performance of the human brain happens when you're twenty or thirty. After that, the mental performance starts to decline gradually. This gradual deterioration is not reversible, but it can be substantially slowed down by an active mental, intellectual, and emotional life during your senior years.

> All I have learned,
> I have learned from books.
> Abraham Lincoln

Most of human mental development comes through formal education during school and college years. But as soon as we leave school, many of us let our minds atrophy. We do not do serious reading anymore, we don't explore new subjects outside of our comfort zone, and we fail to think critically. What do we do instead? We spend lots of time playing screen watching, i.e., staring at all kinds of colored display screens ranging in size from a wristwatch to a giant wall-sized TV screen. What a shame!

Besides being a giant time-waster, the main problem with media watching is that it provides the most potent socializing and cultural influence. And in most cases, this is undesired and unwanted. Why is that? Because we're subject to all value messages transmitted, good or bad, which manipulate us in very subtle, imperceptible, yet powerful ways. Wisdom in watching media requires a smart self-management capacity. That is, to discriminate and select the informing, inspiring, and entertaining programs that best serve and express your purpose and values.

Now let us take a look at the endless possibilities to feed your brain, mind, and intellect on a regular basis:

Education	Information	Other
earn a college degree	watch good quality local, national, and world news	travel
learn a foreign language	go to museums	plant a garden
learn to play a musical instrument	go to art exhibitions and libraries	write a story, poem, or song
learn to write code for mobile apps	watch quality documentaries	observe wildlife

> REMEMBER: NOW YOU HAVE THE
> KNOWHOW AND SELF-DISCIPLINE
> TO CARE FOR YOUR BRAIN, MIND AND INTELLECT.
> GO DO IT!

Caring for Your Heart and Emotional Life

Caring for your heart and emotional life means loving, maintaining great relationships, laughing and being happy.

<u>Love</u>

Love is the most powerful, most elating, and most cherished human emotion. It comes from our Creator, who loves us unconditionally, and asks us to do the same. Love makes people do magnanimous and bold acts, as well as getting themselves in stupid and dangerous situations. But what is love? Love is a higher level of affection and fondness for our Creator and fellow human beings. Depending on the object of the affection, love has several names: *agape* is the divine adoration for our God; *philia* is the brotherly love for fellow men; *storge* is the love for family members, and *eros* is the romantic love for the opposite sex.

Except for divine adoration, earthly love expresses itself in relationships with others in several consistent manners. These manners have been called by Pastor Gary Chapman, *The Five Languages of Love.*[119] You should learn and practice them daily:

1. **Words of Affirmation**: They are phrases that build up the other person: "Honey, you look so beautiful today." "Son, you did such a fine job last week. I'm so proud of you."

2. **Acts of Service:** Always do something for your spouse that you know they would like, such as cooking a meal, washing dishes, going out together on Friday night, etc.

3. **Gifts:** A gift says, 'he was thinking about me,' or 'I love you so much.' The size and value of the present are not significant - what matters is the gesture itself. Bring surprise gifts for spouse and family members when returning from business trips. Always, always celebrate birthdays, anniversaries, and other family occasions with presents and in a festive setting.

4. **Quality Time:** This is the coolest and most effective way to sustain a relationship, yet the easiest forgotten. Make it a habit to spend time with your spouse in a private setting, holding hands, and chatting with each other. Go for long walks in the park together. Have heart-to-heart dialogues as often as possible - they are the oxygen that rekindles the fire of love.

5. **Physical Touch**: Human touch is one of the most powerful expressions of love. Hold hands with your spouse as often as you can, kiss and hug her, and have regular intimate moments together. Be generous with hugs with all other members of the family and close friends.

One should note that most manifestations of the five languages of love can be equally effective in maintaining solid family ties and deep friendships. Some of them can also be very effective in non-family settings, such as a business environment, as well as in sports, arts, and so on.

Relationships

One of the best ways to nourish your heart is to focus on building and maintaining quality relationships. Make daily deposits in your relationship bank account with others by keeping promises, complimenting and encouraging, doing small acts of kindness, being loyal, and listening with your heart. Expect nothing in return; just do it because this is who you are. Look for ways to uplift instead of tear down. Get together often with friends, have fun together, enjoy each other's company. Make new friends as often as opportunities arise.

Renewing our social/emotional dimension does not take as much time as restoring in the other aspects does. We can do it in our regular everyday interactions with other people. But it requires focus and exercise. In the beginning, we may have to push ourselves because we have not yet internalized the necessary skills. But as we get better and better at it, it will become a habit, thus defining us as who we actually are.

Laughing

Why are we so serious-minded? Why do children look so much happier? Perhaps it's because we've been told that laughing is not a grown-up behavior? If this is the case, it's high time to unlearn that bad habit, and acquire a new one: smiling and laughing often! This keeps your heart healthy, strong, and singing. As vocalist Bobby McFerrin[120] puts it in his 1989 Song of the Year and Grammy Award winner: "Don't worry, be happy":

"Here's a little song I wrote
You might want to sing it note for note
Don't worry, be happy
In every life we have some trouble
But when you worry you make it double
Don't worry, be happy
Don't worry, be happy now. "

Follow Bobby's advice to sing your happiness, and you'll definitely get good health, loosening up of the mind, reduced stress, relaxation, connection with others, and joy. So, what are you waiting for?

> **Laughter is**
> **the shortest distance**
> **between two people**
> **Victor Borge**

Learn to laugh at yourself. As someone said, "one of the best things people can have up their sleeve is a good funny bone." Also, remember what feels like a struggle today will bring you strength and enjoyment tomorrow. Be funny with yourself and with others. Bring more laughter in your life by creating your own "humor collection" of books and movies, jokes, YouTube videos, whatever is hilarious to you. When you're feeling low or taking yourself too seriously, visit your collection. Share jokes with friends; encourage them to do the same. Have a good time together, laugh together, make fun of each other. Laughter is contagious, so spread it around!

> REMEMBER: NOW YOU HAVE THE
> KNOWHOW AND SELF-DISCIPLINE
> TO CARE FOR YOUR HEART AND EMOTIONAL LIFE.
> GO DO IT!

Caring for Your Soul and Spiritual Life

The spiritual dimension is the core, the center, the commitment to your Christian value system. It is highly related to stepping stones 1, 2, 3, and 4, which define who you are, i.e., a Christian warrior. The spiritual component is a very private area of life and a crucial one. Christian believers renew their spirituality quite differently. Some people find renewal in daily prayer or meditation on Scriptures, or in closing their eyes and talking to their Creator. Others immerse themselves in great literature, inspiring music, or arts. There are still others who find renewal in the way they engage in the Almighty's creation, for instance, nature. When you're able to leave the noise of the city and give yourself up to the beauty, harmony, and cadence of Mother Nature, you come back renewed spiritually.

> **Create in me a clean heart, O God,**
> **and renew a right spirit within me."**
> **Psalms 51:10**

Spiritual renewal takes an investment of time every day. There is no question that it is a Quadrant II activity, and we really cannot afford to neglect it. It provides leadership to your life; it enforces who you are and the purpose of your journey on this earth. When we take time out to think about the value center of our lives, a good feeling spreads like an umbrella over everything else. It renews us, it refreshes us, and it encourages us to keep going.

Feeding your Soul

Your soul is the most intimate sphere of your life. The soul is that inner self that lies below the surface of your everyday person. The soul is your core, is your treasure chest, where lie your deepest convictions and values. But, also your deepest fears and insecurities. As the famous author and the first American female Noble Laureate for Literature, Pearl S. Buck (1982-1973), wrote: *"Inside myself is a place where I live all alone, and where I find the spiritual springs of water that never dry up. It is also the place wherein its silent chambers, all great battles of life, are being fought."*[121]

Here are a few of the many ways in which people feed their soul:

Meditating and introspection	Praying
Helping others, doing charity	Practicing faith/religion
Reading inspiring books, articles, and blogs	Listening to inspiring music
Reflecting on goals, values, and mission statement	Playing a musical instrument
Writing poetry	Writing in your intimate journal
Talking walks alone	Going into nature

Let's examine closer two of the most loved renewal activities: practicing faith and going into nature.

Practicing faith is a very innermost and fulfilling process of connecting with God regularly. You can do it in the privacy of your room, out in nature, or a place of worship. You can do it alone or together with other believers. When alone, connecting to God should be simple: first, you must have faith; second, be aware that God is waiting for you, and He is patient. Then call on Him; ask Him to accept you in his presence and to listen to your prayers. Meditate on verses from Scriptures such as Hebrews 11:1, "Now faith is the substance of things hoped for, the evidence of things not seen." Express your gratitude for who you are and what you have and ask for continuous guidance and protection in what you do.

Contrary to popular belief, God did not create us all to worship Him in the same way. We're different, not just in our physical appearance and spiritual giftedness, but also in the way we connect with God.[122] And this is a beautiful thing: one body, many parts, and lots of great ways to communicate with the one true God. Figuring out how you connect with God daily is essential to your spiritual life. Our connection comes not from 'what' we do in worship, but 'how' we do it.

Getting back to nature is another excellent way for spiritual renewal. There is something miraculous and uplifting about being in nature. Going back to the natural world means going back to our very human roots. Even if you live in a city far removed from rivers, mountains, or beaches, there will usually be a nearby park or conservation area you can visit. Do it often, preferably once a week. And if possible, go several times a year into the real nature. Visit the untainted places with high mountains, rolling hills, magnificent rivers, and endless seas, to connect back with your ancestry. Where-ever you go, once there, stroll or lay down listening to the birds, to the soft singing of leaves in the wind, or the whispers of water nearby. Watch the clouds unhurriedly crossing the sky, changing shape as they go, or watch a majestic sunset or sunrise. The peace and serenity of those surroundings will make you give thanks to their creator, will calm you down and lift your spirit, and will help recharge your batteries. You will feel if not reborn, at least refreshed.

Avoid A Bad Spiritual Diet

We all know the harmful effects of bad eating habits: people get fat, depressed, and even sick. For this reason, we try to have a healthy nutritional diet to keep us energetic and in good shape. But what are the effects of a bad spiritual diet? What happens if we do not feed our soul properly? To answer these questions, we must first understand what bad spiritual food is. Nowadays, a bad spiritual diet definitely consists of ingesting too much popular culture, spending too much time watching the colored screens of TV, laptops, tablets, smartphones, and video consoles that bring programming content of questionable quality. A bad spiritual diet means letting yourself be mesmerized by the dark side of technology, without realizing the terrible impact it may have on your soul.

Remember, you're not only what you eat, but you're also what you listen to, read, and see. More important than what goes into your body is what goes into your soul. Why is this? Because if you listen to bad language, see violent behavior, and have negative thoughts, your soul becomes dark, angry, and violent. As a result, your whole subjective world becomes dark, angry, and violent. You will live in a realm that does not actually exist except in your head and soul. Cinema and literature can change our lives in noble and profound ways.[123] They can, but usually don't. For every The Patriot and Doctor Zhivago film that enriches and inspires us, you get three sequels of Jaws, two chapters of It and countless other horror movies which tear us down.

How to separate proper spiritual diet from trash? Very simply: if you watch something that uplifts you and makes you feel optimistic and passionate, that is a good quality diet. However, if it makes you depressed, scared, negative, and angry - that is trash for your soul.

How powerful and toxic are the messages about values that young people are receiving from popular media today? According to a large body of research,[124] the answer is 'very.' The study demonstrates that wrong values actually hurt children. Such bad values include: success at any cost, wealth and materialism, fame, and excessive sexuality. They affect the way teen-agers think of themselves and how they associate with others. They want to imitate rock stars and celebrities. Success at any cost makes models of dishonesty, cheating, back-stabbing, and manipulation not only acceptable but even desirable. And this is not tolerable!

Balance your Spiritual Life

What does it mean to balance your spiritual life? What does it mean to balance your life in general? Well, to answer these questions, we must go back to the teachings of Pastor Rick Warren. He tells us that the Christian life is a pentathlon of five purposes that must be kept in balance.[125] These five purposes are: (i) love your God, (ii) love your neighbors, (iii) go and make disciples, (iv) live in God's family, and finally, (v) become like Christ.

Keeping these five purposes in balance is not easy. Actually, it is hard, because we also have to keep in balance the demands of our worldly life. For these reasons, Pastor Warren advises us to join a small group of believers who have the same aims. Joining the group will help you stay on track by doing the following:

- Talk it through with your spiritual partners in the group. The best way to internalize the five purposes of life is to discuss them, debate them, and even argue about them in a private setting.

- Give yourself a regular spiritual checkup. This means to evaluate yourself periodically sincerely and objectively. Are you on track? Are you getting better in all five areas, or are you ignoring some?

- Write down your progress in an intimate journal. Writing your thoughts in a faith journal will help you see clearly what God is doing in your life. It will let you assess the progress—or lack of it – from one year to another, allowing you to take corrective actions.

- Pass on what you know to others. If you want to keep growing, you must start teaching others what you have learned. Those who pass along their insights get more from God, and therefore grow spiritually.

Balancing your spiritual life means to make the rest of your life the best it can be, regardless of your age or station in life. Balancing your spiritual life means glorifying God and helping grow his kingdom.

REMEMBER: MAKE DAILY SPIRITUAL RENEWAL
THE FOUNDATION OF YOUR CHRISTIAN FAITH

Standing on Stepping Stone 5

Stepping Stone 5 is where you have added and polished new facets to your Diamond Soul character. Mostly, you have learned how to deal with the world around you based on the Christian virtues of Patience, Justice, and Kindness. Dealing with the world around you means understanding the complexities of human relationships and learning how to build and maintain long-lasting and meaningful ones. Further down, we will identify the four great victories you have achieved by standing on this platform of learning. The first three victories relate to constructing and maintaining effective human relationships by thinking mutual advantage, using the art of persuasion, and applying the principle of creative cooperation. The fourth victory relates to investing in the most critical asset you have - you- by being faithful to your daily rejuvenation practices.

First Victory: Always Think Win-Win

The capacity to think Win-Win is the result of respecting your fellow humans and having an abundance mentality. Now you realize the importance of nurturing, building, and developing relationships based on mutual trust and respect. You also know how to maintain them by making daily deposits in the relationship bank account, and how to repair them when they start deteriorating. You make sense of all possible combinations of the win-lose matrix and comprehend why the 'Win-Win or no deal' is the best solution under most circumstances.

Second Victory: Mastering the Art of Influencing Others

You have learned that influencing others means having a Diamond Soul character and possessing practical communication skills. You know that the Golden Rule for productive communications is to listen first and talk later. Listening first gives you the ability to enter into your interlocutor's mind and heart to understand his deep emotions and feelings. During this process, a strange yet miraculous experience takes place; the mutual influence. Then, as you speak with passion, you expose your point of view. When doing it, use the age-old concept of ethos, pathos, and logos, which lets your character first establish authority (ethos), use emotion to open the heart of the listener (pathos), and finally speak passionately to make you rational case (logos). Before speaking to small or larger groups, you know how to prepare, structure, and deliver your speech for maximum impact.

Third Victory: Mastering the Art of Creative Cooperation

Third victory relates to the art of creative cooperation, or the habit of thinking and acting synergistically. You have learned how to value differences between people and how to embrace diversity. When dealing with differences, now you know that besides those evident, there are plenty of hidden ones that need to be identified and understood respectfully and skillfully. Whenever you think cooperation, you immediately ask the question: 'How can I make it synergistic?' You always look for the higher way, or the third alternative, whenever problems or opportunities arise.

Fourth Victory: Daily Rejuvenation

This is the new capacity to be true to your daily rejuvenation programs and apply them in all measures of human existence: body, mind, emotion, and spirit. This is how you invest in your greatest assets, yourself. To maintain your body in top shape, you eat properly, get enough sleep and have a fitness program. You care for your intellect and mind by staying curious, learning new skills, and being informed. You maintain a healthy emotional life by having good relationships, going out in nature, and remaining positive. And finally, your spiritual rejuvenation is expressed through daily moments of introspection, prayers and devotion, and participation in the activities of the church to which you belong.

Moments of Reflection

1. What's the importance of daily renewal?

2. What does your body need to function correctly?

3. What makes proper nutrition? Describe myPlate nutritional guidelines.

4. What are the effects of eating too much junk food? How do you change poor eating habits?

5. Describe a balanced morning exercise program.

6. What are your favorite outdoor activities?

7. What does rejuvenating the intellect mean?

8. How much screen time do you spend each day?

9. What are you doing right now to further your education?

10. How do you renew your emotional life?

11. How do you care for your Soul?

12. How often do you try to connect to God? How do you do it?

13. What is an adequate diet for your soul?

14. What's your favorite way of renewing your spirit?

15. What did you learn on Stepping Stone 5?

16. Which are the four victories you have achieved in doing so?

CHAPTER 19
THE JOY OF SERVING OTHERS

—•+•◆•+•—

"But all these worketh that one and the
self-same Spirit, dividing to every man
severally as he will. (1 Corinthians 12:11)

The Humble Servant

"For even the Son of man came not to be ministered unto, but to
minister, and to give his life as a ransom for many." (Mark 10:45)

P astor Rick Warren teaches us that "*We bring God glory by serving
others*".[126] While the world measures greatness in terms of power,
possessions, and prestige, Jesus measures greatness in terms of service and
humility. He determines your status by how many people you serve, not
how many people are in your employment.

Most of us Christians want to serve because we know it is our duty. But
how many of us do it with passion and joy? How many of us do it day in and
day out? Most people think that Christians should serve only Christians.
While this is true and noble, it is not what Jesus did during his ministry on
Earth. Jesus served the Jews and Gentiles alike, the underclass, the meek,

the sick, the poor and the lepers, the destitute people he encountered during his travels, not in the temple.

> **The disciple is not above his master:**
> **but every one that is perfect**
> **shall be as his master.**
> **Luke 6:40**

Our obligation to serve the church is enshrined in us being Christians, and we must do our best to do it. This is our ministry. But the hours per week spent at church or in the companion of fellow believers are really small compared with the hours we spend at work and with the family. There is a much larger field of opportunities to serve others at work, with neighbors, friends, and family. This is our mission.

These well-known principles of servanthood should guide everyone aspiring to become a humble servant:

Service starts in your head and heart: You must put others ahead of yourself. In the beginning, use your head to make this choice, but as your humility increases, your heart will tell you what to do. It should be the Christian virtue of love deeply engrained in your Diamond Soul character that drives your service, not your calculations.

Start serving today, not tomorrow: Start with your family in the morning, at work during the day, at the baseball game or Bible study class in the afternoon, and with your friends in the evening. Remember, in the beginning; you are a beginner, so you must train yourself; you must go through the apprenticeship of service. The earlier you start, the sooner you'll get good at it. If you can start with someone you know, perfect; if not, start on your own. But start today!

What to do on the first day of service: Do what you did yesterday, but better, with more passion, with more joy. Talk more often, in a friendlier manner, and with a bigger smile on your face with all the people around you. If you see someone stumbling, jump right ahead to help. If you see someone sad, go and listen to her problems. Ask your kids how they did at school; offer help with homework assignments, and so on. The opportunities are endless.

Forget that you have weaknesses: We all do. We all are beginners at some point in time. The good news is that God loves to use weak people to do his work. If God were to use only perfect and fully trained people, his work would never get done. We, the weak and untrained people, are his army. We do his work the best we can, with what we have around us, and at our pace. The strength of God's army is in the millions of us able and willing to serve.

Look around for service opportunities. In the beginning, you see service as something separate from your daily activities, and you will look for such opportunities around you. And this is good, because you must train your eye to spot other people's needs. Once you have identified a need, jump in to fulfill it, regardless if it is menial or grandiose. This would become your field of service for the day, the week, or the month. But later on, as you gather more experience, you will realize that service should not be only something unusual outside of your daily routines. Your daily routines should become something special and be done in a spirit of service with equal dedication, dignity, and joy.

Give yourself to others expecting nothing in return. You do not act generously to impress or to buy favor with others. Your generosity is who you are, how you behave. The Bible tells us in Luke 6:38, "Give, and it shall be given unto you...For with the same measure that ye mete withal it shall be measured to you again." But your reward comes not from the person you serve, but from Christ himself. You will receive a spiritual compensation later on for a really good deed you do now.

Become and remain humble. Since all of us are sinners, we must force ourselves into humility to become humble. At least in the beginning. Our innate sinful pride will be the main stumbling block on the road to grow in humility. That's why we continuously need the guidance and support of the Holy Spirit. Of course, we must be mindful and proud of the good deeds we're doing and help others to do the same. But we don't do it for worldly praise or recognition; we do it for the glory of God. And we do it in all the humility of which we're capable.

Be a light for others. At home, encourage everyone to embark on the road of servanthood to each other. In Peter 5:5, the apostle instructs us "… Likewise, ye younger, submit yourselves unto the elder. Yea, all *of you* be subject one to another, and be clothed with humility: for God resisteth the proud, and giveth grace to the humble." Be a light to all around you. To those who are eager to serve, provide guidance and inspiration. With those who are reluctant to help, be patient, but persistent. Teach, admonish, and discipline as required, and as the Holy Spirit guides you. Always keep in mind that your deeds and moral authority speak louder than your words, so let them shine. The same principles apply equally well in a work setting: influence others to enter the field of unselfish service by you being a selfless and humble servant.

Train others as humble servants. Identify, train, encourage, and inspire other believers to follow into Jesus's steps of humble servanthood. Take younger people with you when you are on a mission. Coach, mentor, and support them. When other people ignore or ridicule you, carry on. Don't get discouraged; keep doing it for the glory of the Almighty.

The Upward Spiral

"Verily, verily, I say unto you, He that believeth on me, the works that I do shall he do also…." (John 14:12)

REMEMBER: BECOME A JOYFUL AND
HUMBLE SERVANT AS JESUS WAS DURING
HIS MINISTRIES ON EARTH

This is how Geoff Ward[127] talks about the spiral as the organizing principle at work in the universe:

"So, spiral energy fields are all around us and within us, patterning our very existence, from microcosm to macrocosm, determining structures from the tiny vortices of sub-atomic particles and the DNA molecule to the awesome island universes of galaxies where stars are born, and the conditions for life created.

Indeed, the protean spiral is nature's most favored pattern of growth and the most efficacious deployer of its energy — life-inducing, life-protecting, and life-supporting. Ultimately, the implication is that the spiral form is integral to strength and growth, and indeed, it may be that all curves of growth are based on it. It is a powerful example of how nature tends to repeat the use of a successful design over and over again on every level of its creative handiwork."

In almost every culture, the shape associated with growth is the spiral. This is because many things in nature grow in spirals, from ferns to seashells to whirlpools. Spirals can be as small as the double helix of a protein molecule and as large as the spiral arms of the Milky Way galaxy. The spiral is simply the shape created by a self-reinforcing growth process. By definition, a spiral winds around a center, in a progressive expansion or contraction, a rise or fall, in an upward direction or a downward course.

We tend to associate an upward spiral with growth, development, and evolution. In contrast, a descending spiral is associated with decline, slowdown, and retreat. We use the metaphor of the ascending spiral to describe the process of self-growth and continuous positive transformation in one's life. As such, the spiral becomes a process of mutually reinforcing changes that create something we value at higher and higher levels. And what do we value? Of course, it must be our value system, our Diamond Soul character, and the principles of conduct that define us. Our valuables are embodied in feelings of happiness, empowerment, abundance, integrity, and drawing closer to God.

Walking up the self-growth spiral becomes most effective if done daily. If we do not renew daily, if we do not maintain a positive attitude, we will stagnate first, then slowly but surely go down the slippery slope of an emotional spiral. It is a downward process that is easy to start and difficult to stop. It begins with boredom, frustration, pessimism, and disappointment, followed by worries, blames, discouragement, and anger. After anger comes hatred, jealousy, and desire for revenge. It ends up with insecurities, guilt, fear, and depression. The descending emotional spiral takes you down to where no human being wants to be, but many end up being, in the dark world of depression and emotional confusion.

In contrast, an optimistic soul, under the guidance of the Holy Spirit and supported by a daily renewal process, will put you on the never-ending ascending path of personal development and spiritual growth. We can visualize it as an ascending spiral starting from hopefulness and calm optimism and going upwards forever. It begins with feelings of contentment, serenity, and positive expectations. They, sooner or later, become fervor for what you do, passion for living, and confidence. Keep pushing up, and you will find yourself in the realm of perpetual joy, freedom, and unconditional love. This spiral takes you where you want to be, closer and closer to Christ!

> REMEMBER: CLIMBING UP DAILY ON THE
> ASCENDING SPIRAL OF PERSONAL AND
> SPIRITUAL GROWTH TAKES YOU
> CLOSER AND CLOSER TO GOD

Your Tremendous Diamond Soul Character

As seen in previous chapters, climbing the first four stepping stones has led you to acquire a Diamond Soul character. You now know what it means to be a Christian and a Righteous Warrior in Christ. You have determined your godly way in life, and you have taught yourself self-discipline. These are the first facets of your new Diamond Soul character. It took time and lots of effort to cut and polish them, but now you stand on the solid foundation of a Christlike character. This new Diamond Soul character defines the new you now and describes the different individual you have become under the guidance of the Holy Spirit. In sum, now you know who you are, where you want to go, and how to get there.

But you did not stop there: by scaling the remaining Stepping Stone 5, you have entered into the marvelous yet still mysterious world of human relationships. By learning and internalizing the teachings found on this platform of learning, you have added a few more facets to your Diamond Soul character, thus making it beautiful, tremendous, and whole. These new facets represent your recently acquired skills in thinking win-win, in the art of influencing others, and in becoming a determined synergizer. These also represent your new abilities to deal with people of all walks of life in a trusting, respectful, and courageous way. This means that you are not only a man of character; you have also become a wise man and a leader.

Now that the shaping of your character is complete, how can you best describe it? How do you answer the question, *"which are the most important traits of your character?"* or *"what do you call the most important facets of your Diamond Soul?"* Answers to these questions are very personal because they define your uniqueness. For instance, let's assume that you are a person of middle age. If this is the case, you may elect to represent yourself through seven beautifully cut and polished facets of your Diamond Soul character. These facets may be industry, integrity, wisdom, leadership, modesty, love, and service.

1. Industry: your capacity to work hard and with joy.

2. Integrity: your commitment to be true to yourself and others.

3. Wisdom: your wisdom is based on Christian wisdom.

4. Leadership: you lead by personal example.

5. Modesty: you are humble before the Lord and all His creation.

6. Love: as your Creator loves you unconditionally, you, too, like others unconditionally.

7. Service: your service to others comes from your heart, with no expectation of reciprocity.

> REMEMBER: YOUR ARE NOW BLESSED
> WITH A TREMENDOUS AND WHOLESOME
> DIAMOND SOUL CHARACTER
> INSPIRED BY THE HOLLY SPIRIT.
> TAKE GOOD CARE OF IT!

Moments of Reflection

1. Which are the principles of servanthood?

2. Why should we all aspire to become humble servants?

3. Describe the benefits of climbing up on the ascending spiral.

4. Contrast the ascending spiral with a downward spiral

5. Which is the foundation of your Diamond Soul character?

6. Describe several desired facets of your new Diamond Soul character.

For Further Reading

—◆·◆·◆·◆—

Chapman, Garry: *The Five Languages of Love - The secret to love that lasts*, Northfield Publishing, 2010.

Clear, James: *Atomic Habits*, Penguin Random House, 2018

Covey, Stephen R.: *The Seven Habits of Highly Effective People*, Kindle Edition, Infographics edition, Mango Publishing, 2015

Frankl, Viktor E.: *Man's Search for Meaning*, Beacon Press, 2006

Hall, Calvin S.: *A Primer of Freudian Psychology*, Mentor, 1954.

Jones, Tracy C.: *Beyond Tremendous- Raising the Bar on Life*, Tremendous Life Books, 2015.

Maxwell, John C. *Becoming a Person of Influence*, Thomas Nelson, 1997.

Munroe, Myles: *The Power of Character in Leadership*, Whitaker House, 2017

Parrot, Les: *Love Like That - 5 relationship secrets from Jesus*, Nelson Books, 2018.

Robins, Anthony: *Awaken the Giant Within*, Firestone, 1991.

Sanders, J. Oswald: *Cultivation of Christian Character*, Moody Publishers, 1965.

Seligman, M. and Peterson, C.: *Character, Strength and Virtues*, American Psychological Association, Oxford University Press, 2004.

Warren, Rick: *The Purpose Driven Life*, Zondervan, 2018.

ABOUT THE AUTHOR

G eorge Vasilca writes on topics related to self-help, moral character improvement, and leadership. His audience is Christian men and women interested in continuous personal development and spiritual growth.

George is a retired professional engineer and business executive with over forty-five years of experience in business leadership, project management, and technology development. He has a multi-cultural background and international business experience. He has been a facilitator of technical collaboration and technology transfer programs, and business partnerships. For many years, George has been mentoring young leaders with a particular focus on developing a solid moral character, enhancing the effectiveness of human relations, and refining the principles of leadership and management.

George received his Master of Science degree in Electrical Engineering from the University Politechnica in Bucharest, Romania. After working for a few years in his native country, George moved to West Germany, then immigrated to Canada in 1974. He held senior positions with several multi-national companies, then started his own engineering firm in

Toronto, Ontario. In 1991, George moved to the US to become a founding director and executive officer of the Casmyn Vector Group of Sparks, NV. From the mid-nineties until his retirement, George provided consulting engineering and project management services to Hershey Corporation of Hershey, PA.

George is a licensed Professional Engineer (ret) in the US and Canada, a retired member of several professional organizations, and a life member of the Institute of Electrical and Electronics Engineers. He is the recipient of several awards from professional organizations and other entities.

His interests focus on the importance of faith in contemporary America, the history of Christianity, ethics and morality, and application of the latest scientific findings in psychology and human behavior. George lives with his wife Mara, also a writer, in Hershey, PA. He has two grown-up sons and one grandson.

George writes regularly for his blog located on his author website www.georgevasilca.org.

ENDNOTES

———◦◦◦———

1   Sir Ernest Shakleton, Wikipedia.org, accessed 12/10/2019

2   Virtues, Webster Dictionary online, accessed 05/10/2020

3   Seven Virtues, Wikipedia.org, accessed 12/19/1019

4   Agape, Wikipedia.org, accessed 12/19/1019

5   Justice and Rights of Man, Wikipedia.org, accessed 12/19/1019

6   Vice, Wikipedia.org, accessed 12/19/1019

7   Seven Deadly Sins, Wikipedia.org, accessed 12/19/1019

8   Moral character, Webster Dictionary online, accessed 05/10/2020

9   Character of man, Wikipedia.org, accessed 12/19/1019

10 Sanders, Oswald, *Cultivation of Christian Character*, Moody Press, 2019, p.83, 84

11 Preacher Charles E. Jefferson, *On Character of Jesus*, lectures delivered at Broadway Tabernacle Church, New York City, in 1908. Published in BiblioBazaar, 2012, p.25

12 Patience, Webster Dictionary online, accessed 05/10/2020

13 Rick Warren, *The Purpose Driven Life*, Kindle Edition, Zondervan, 2018, p.307

14 Rick Warren, *The Purpose Driven Life*, Kindle Edition, Zondervan, 2018, p.30

15 Preacher Charles E. Jefferson, *On Character of Jesus*, lectures delivered at Broadway Tabernacle Church, New York City, in 1908. Published in BiblioBazaar, 2012, p.27

16   Plato, Wikipedia.org, accessed 12/19/2019

17   Self-knowledge (psychology), Wikipedia.org, accessed 12/19/2019

18   Composition of the human body, Wikipedia.org, accessed 12/19/2019

19   Conscience, Wikipedia.org, accessed 12/19/2019

20   Bradley Voytek, Are there as many neurons…, Nature.com, accessed 12/19/2019

21   Neuroplasticity, Wikipedia.org, accessed 12/19/2019

22   Emotions, Webster Dictionary online, accessed 05/10/2020

23   Id, ego, superego, Wikipedia.org, accesses 05/10/2020

24   Spirituality, Webster Dictionary online, accessed 05/10/2020

25   Steven R. Covey, *The Seven Habits of Highly Effective People*, Kindle Edition, Infographics edition, Mango Publishing, 2015, p.97

26   Viktor E. Frankl, *Man's Search for Meaning*, Beacon Press, 2006

27   Epigenetics, Wikipedia.org, accessed 12/19/2019

28   Steven R. Covey, *The Seven Habits of Highly Effective People*, Kindle Edition, Infographics edition, Mango Publishing, 2015, p.6

29   Pareto principle, Wikipedia.org, accesses 05/10/2020

30   James Clear, How long does it take…, Jameshabit.com, accessed 12/19/2019

31   Influence, Webster Dictionary online, accessed 05/10/2020

32   Circle of Influence and …, podcast, Theteachingspace.com, accessed 12/19/2019

33   Integrity, Webster Dictionary online, accessed 05/10/2020

34   Courage, Webster Dictionary online, accessed 05/10/2020

35   Rick Warren, *The Purpose Driven Life*, Kindle Edition, Zondervan, 2018, p.74

36   Viktor E. Frankl, *Man's Search for Meaning*, Beacon Press, 2006, p.66

37   Billy Graham Evangelistic Association, Billygraham.org, accessed 12/19/2019

38   Stay on God's path, Jan.7/ 2008, Proverbs31.org, accessed 12/19/2019

39   Aristotle, Wikipedia.org, accessed 12/19/2019

40   US Flight 1544, Wikipedia.org, accessed 12/19/2019

41   B. Radford, Does the human body replaces..., 04/04/2011, accessed 12/19/2019

42   Robert Frost, The Road not Taken, thepoetryfoundation.org, accessed 12/19/2019

43   Peter Drucker, Wikipedia.org, accessed 12/19/2019

44   William Shakespeare, Wikipedia.org, accessed 12/19/2019

45   Mission in life, Webster Dictionary online, accessed 05/10/2020

46   Inner gifts, Naturalgiftssociety.org, accesses 05/10/2020

47   Three ways to figure out..., Themuse.com, accessed 12/19/2019

48   Marcel Schwantes, Study: 60 percent of workers...., Inc.com, accessed 12/19/2019

49   Personal mission statements, Fastcompany.com, accessed 12/19/2019

50   B&K McKay, Creating a positive family..., 05/27/2018, Artofmanliness.com, accessed 12/20/2019

51   Three kernels of corn, 12/ 2/ 2011, Betterlifecoachingblog.com, accessed 12/19/2019

52   Riches, wealth, Webster Dictionary online, accessed 05/10/2020

53   What is wealth building? Handsonbanking.com, accessed 12/19/2019

54   Destiny, Tonyevans.org, accessed 05/10/2020

55   Destiny, Webster Dictionary online, accessed 05/10/2020

56   Fate and destiny, lonerwolf.com, accessed 05/10/2020

57   John McCain, *Character is Destiny*, Random House, 2005, p.7

58   Heraclitus, Wikipedia.org, accessed 12/20/2019

59   Alexis de Tocqueville, Wikipedia.org, accessed 12/20/2019

60   Theodore Roosevelt, Wikipedia.org, accessed 12/20/2019

61   Samuel Smiles, Wikipedia.org, accessed 12/20/2019

62   Ralph Drollinger, Wikipedia.org, accessed 12/20/2019

63   Time is priceless..., 12-13-2013, Keyisinspiration.com, accessed 12/19/2019

64   Rick Warren, *The Purpose Driven Life*, Kindle Edition, Zondervan, 2018, p.199

65   Definition of time, Exactlywhatistime.com, accessed 12/19/2019

66   Albert Einstein, Wikipedia.org, accessed 12/20/2019

67   Plato, Wikipedia.org, accessed 12/19/2019

68   Augustine of Hippo, Wikipedia.org, accessed 12/19/2019

69   John Harrison, Wikipedia.org, accessed 12/19/2019

70   Greenwich Mean Time, Wikipedia.org, accessed 12/19/2019

71   Time management, Wikipedia.org, accessed 12/19/2019

72   Dwight Eisenhower, Wikipedia.org, accessed 12/19/2019

73   Eisenhower method, Wikipedia.org, accessed 12/19/2019

74   Richard Koch, Wikipedia.org, accessed 12/19/2019

75   A story of priorities, 02-24-2004, Sparkpeople.com, accessed 12/19/2019

76   Urgent, Webster Dictionary online, accessed 05/10/2020

77   Important, Webster Dictionary online, accessed 05/10/2020

78   Eisenhower Urgent/Important Principle, Mindtools.com, accessed 12/20/2019

79   Priorities, Webster Dictionary online, accessed 05/10/2020

80   Socrates, Wikipedia.org, accessed 12/19/2019

81   Time management skills, Indeed.com, accessed 12/20/2019

82   Ten characteristics... go.psmj.com, blog, accessed 12/20/2019

83   How to say no, Scienceofpeople.com, accessed 12/20/2019

84   How to say no to temptation, Skilledlife.com, accessed 12/20/2019

85   Lisa McQuarrey: Principles of self-management, Workchron.com, accessed 12/20/2019

86   Liz Ryan: ten ways to step out of your comfort zone, Forbes.com, accessed 12/20/2019

87   Delegation, Webster Dictionary online, accessed 05/10/2020

88   Alex Czarto: Stewardship Delegation, Czarto.com, accessed 12/20/2019

89   Stephen Hawking's Life, 03/15/2018, timesofindia.com, accessed 12/19/2019

90   Free Will, Wikipedia.org, accessed 12/19/2019

91   What is Willpower? Changingminds.org, accessed 12/19/2019

92 Remez Sasson: What is self-discipline, Successconsciousness.com accessed 12/19/2019

93 The law of entropy, Wikipedia.org, accessed 12/19/2019

94 Oksana Tunikova: The science of willpower, Medium.com, accessed 12/19/2019

95 Seth S. Horowitz, The Science and Art of Listening, New York Times, 11/ 9/2012

96 Valerie Brown, 'What happens when…, 06/21/2016, Couragerenewal. org, acc. 12/19/ 2019

97 Trust (psychology), Wikipedia.org, accessed 12/19/2019

98 Steven R. Covey, *The Seven Habits of Highly Effective People*, Kindle Edition, Infographics edition, Mango Publishing, 2015, p.294

99 Frenchpdf.com, seven habits, Internetarchive.com, accessed 12/19/2019

100 Think Win-Win, Gbnews.ch, accessed 12/19/2019

101 John C. Maxwell, *Becoming a Person of Influence*, Nelson Publishing, 1997, p.96

102 John C. Maxwell, *Developing the Leader within You*, Nelson Publishing, 1993, p.33

103 Jeanne Segal, Ph.D., Nonverbal Communications, helpguide.com, accessed 12/20/2019

104 Charles Swindoll, Dialogue of the deaf, Sept. 2015, insight.org, accessed 12/20/2019

105 Steven R. Covey, *The Seven Habits of Highly Effective People*, Kindle Edition, Infographics edition, Mango Publishing, 2015, p.388

106 Depth of Listening, Changingminds.org, accessed 12/20/2019

107 Heart-to-Heart Dialogue, Yourlisteningbody.com, accessed 12/20/2019

108 Modes of Persuasion, Pathosethoslogos.com, accessed 12/20/2019

109 Five ways to speak passionately, Fastcompany.com, accessed 12/20/2019

110 Introduction to interpersonal communications, Pearsonhighered.

com, accessed 12/20/2019

111   Diversity, Qcc.cuny.edu, accessed 12/19/2019

112   Synergy, Wikipedia.org, accessed 12/19/2019

113   Social interdependence, Systemsinnovation.io, accessed 12/19/2019

114   Steven R. Covey, *The Seven Habits of Highly Effective People*, Kindle Edition, Infographics edition, Mango Publishing, 2015, p.427

115   Cathy Jacobs, Ten simple habits…, Fireinside.com, 03/24/2017, accessed 12/19/2019

116   USDA MyPlate, Choosemyplate.gov, accessed 12/19/2019

117   Fitness training: elements of a well-balanced…, Mayoclinic.org, accessed 12/19/2019

118   Healthy sleep tips, Sleepfoundation.org, accessed 12/19/2019

119   Garry Chapman: Understanding the five…, Focusonthefamily.com, accessed 12/19/2019

120   Bobby McFerrin, Wikipedia.org, accessed 12/19/2019

121   Pearl S. Buck, Wikipedia.org, accessed 12/19/2019

122   The ultimate guide…Onethingalone.com, accessed 12/19/2019

123   Six disastrous ways…, Cracked.com, accessed 12/19/2019

124   Jim Taylor, Ph.D.: Media teaches bad values... Psychologytoday.com, accessed 12/19/ 2019

125   Rick Warren, *The Purpose Driven Life*, Kindle Edition, Zondervan, 2018, p.365

126   Rick Warren, *The Purpose Driven Life*, Kindle Edition, Zondervan, 2018, p.95

127   Geoff Ward, Spirals: the patterns of …. Medium.com, 03/01/2018, accessed 12/19/2019